Expert
Network Time
Protocol

An Experience in Time
with NTP

PETER RYBACZYK

Apress®

Expert Network Time Protocol: An Experience in Time with NTP

Copyright © 2005 by Peter Rybaczyk

Lead Editor: Jim Sumser
Technical Reviewer: Jim Cornelson
Editorial Board: Steve Anglin, Dan Appleman, Ewan Buckingham, Gary Cornell, Tony Davis,
   Jason Gilmore, Jonathan Hassell, Chris Mills, Dominic Shakeshaft, Jim Sumser
Assistant Publisher: Grace Wong
Project Manager: Sofia Marchant
Copy Manager: Nicole LeClerc
Copy Editor: Kim Wimpsett
Production Manager: Kari Brooks-Copony
Production Editors: Kari Brooks-Copony, Kelly Winquist
Compositor: Linda Weidemann
Proofreader: Liz Welch
Indexer: Carol Burbo
Artist: April Milne
Cover Designer: Kurt Krames
Manufacturing Manager: Tom Debolski

Library of Congress Cataloging-in-Publication Data

Rybaczyk, Peter.
  Expert Network Time Protocol / Peter Rybaczyk.
    p. cm.
  Includes bibliographical references.
  ISBN 1-59059-484-3
  1. Network Time Protocol (Computer network protocol) I. Title.

TK5105.575R93 2005
004.6'2--dc22
                        2005013042

Distributed to the book trade in the United States by Springer-Verlag New York, Inc., 233 Spring Street, 6th Floor, New York, NY 10013, and outside the United States by Springer-Verlag GmbH & Co. KG, Tiergartenstr. 17, 69112 Heidelberg, Germany.

In the United States: phone 1-800-SPRINGER, fax 201-348-4505, e-mail orders@springer-ny.com, or visit http://www.springer-ny.com. Outside the United States: fax +49 6221 345229, e-mail orders@springer.de, or visit http://www.springer.de.

For information on translations, please contact Apress directly at 2560 Ninth Street, Suite 219, Berkeley, CA 94710. Phone 510-549-5930, fax 510-549-5939, e-mail info@apress.com, or visit http://www.apress.com.

To Jim Sumser

Contents at a Glance

PART 1 ■ ■ ■ NTP: The Key to Time Transcendence

PART 2 ■ ■ ■ NTP: The Story Behind the Accuracy and Synchronization of Network Time

Contents

PART 1 ■■■ NTP: The Key to Time Transcendence

PART 2 ■■■ **NTP: The Story Behind the Accuracy and Synchronization of Network Time**

About the Author

PETER RYBACZYK is an internetworking consultant, a technical author, an IT seminar conductor, and a business owner. He began his IT career as an application programmer, database administrator, and network administrator for the Summit University Press publishing house during the 1980s. After starting his first consulting business in 1990, he worked with telecom equipment vendors (Nortel Networks, Ericsson, Cisco Systems), local and regional ISPs, VoIP providers, law firms, health care providers, auto dealerships, and banks. Rybaczyk has designed, installed, and managed numerous LANs and WANs in diverse multiprotocol environments. And he has delivered more than 120 IT seminars worldwide. Earlier in the decade, he was involved for two years in the design, deployment, configuration, and management of a nationwide VoIP network in the United States.

During his training career, Rybaczyk has conducted seminars on VoIP, routing protocols (OSPF and BGP), the TCP/IP protocol suite, Cisco routers and switches, network management, WAN switches, and data networks design and optimization. He has developed custom training courses on Cisco WAN management products, OSPF, rapid development tools, and VoIP that he has delivered to audiences in the United States, Canada, Europe, Australia, and Asia. He is a former Certified Cisco Systems Instructor (CCSI) and was the master of ceremonies at VoIP Congress 2003 in Singapore and VoIP Congress 2004 in Kuala Lumpur.

Rybaczyk has a bachelor's degree in physics from the University of Missouri–St. Louis. He also holds several industry certifications including CNE, CCNA, and CCNP. Rybaczyk's IT consulting firm, Convergent Netcom Services, is located in Tucson, Arizona.

About the Technical Reviewer

 **JIM CORNELSON** is currently a network engineer for SurveySampling. He has worked as a network engineer for two school districts and as a project manager for a VoIP startup. In previous lives, he taught technology for five years to seventh and eighth graders and worked a series of construction jobs, including working the eight-month winter in McMurdo, Antarctica, in 1987. His wife, Michelle; his son, Jesse; and his Cisco lab provide hours of entertainment while at home. He has a bachelor's degree in philosophy from Oklahoma State University, and he currently holds certification as a CCNA, CCDA, CCNP, CCDP, and CWNA.

Acknowledgments

A phenomenal amount of professional expertise and personal dedication was required on the part of many individuals to bring this book to fruition. The project began with Jim Sumser holding the vision that a book on the subject of NTP could be done. Thank you, Jim! Outlines, proposals, and editorial reviews followed. The easy part came next: writing. Then, an amazing-to-behold team effort kicked in: technical and development reviews, revisions and corrections, copyediting, layout, composition, proofing, and more reviews. Thank you to everyone who has been a part of this process whether I had the opportunity to work with you directly or not.

Many thanks to my technical editor, Jim Cornelson, for your insights and dedication in pointing out those areas of the manuscript that required corrections and greater clarity. Special thanks to Kim Wimpsett for a superprofessional and considerate approach to copyediting. Many thanks to Sofia Marchant for managing the entire project and keeping me on track with manuscript and review deliveries. A big thank you to Tina Nielsen, Kari Brooks-Copony, Kelly Winquist, and Julie Miller for your parts in the administration, production, and marketing of this book.

A very special thank you to Paul Skoog from Symmetricom for taking time out of your busy schedule to grant me an interview and share your insights on the subject of NTP, provide information about Symmetricom's products, and supply pictures of Symmetricom's timeserver and configuration screens that appear in Chapter 5. Thank you to Raychel Marcotte of BroadPR for arranging the interview with Paul and for all the subsequent follow-up. While I've had this opportunity to write on the subject of NTP, there is one individual whom everyone in the NTP community recognizes as the pioneer in this field: Dr. David L. Mills from the University of Delaware. Thank you, Dr. Mills, for your efforts over the last two decades and more on behalf of advancing this protocol. Without you, there would be no NTP!

It is also a pleasure to acknowledge family members and friends who've cheered me on and offered encouragement and support not only during this effort but also in the years and months leading to it. Thank you to Mom and Dad, Elizabeth, Gieniek, Barbara, John, Dorothy, Pramod, Maureen, Dan, James, Bogdan, Leszek, Kelly, Czarek, Asia, Ania, Rachel, Lawrence, Karen, Thomas, Anthony, and Peter. Thank you to Barbara and Clyde, Guy and Marie, Edward and Eileen, Andrew and Kathleen, Andres and Kathleen, George and JoAnn, Sheila and Steve, and Cindy and Jack for the sustaining bonds of friendship that, appropriately enough given the subject of this book, seem to transcend time.

Thank you, Maria! You know that without your love and support this book would not have happened! Last but not least, thank you, Yeshe and Jacques, for your companionship and the comfort you offered during this writing project.

Introduction

Time permeates every facet of modern-day computing and networking. It is also an integral element of everyday living. And it's a given that most networking professionals have at one time or another encountered and/or configured NTP, even if without fully understanding the science of accurate and synchronized timekeeping behind it.

You do not need NTP at all if you are satisfied with networks where every internal and external clock ticks to its own rhythm, keeping track of time independent of all the other clocks. You can also navigate throughout your entire networking career with a limited understanding of NTP when accurate timekeeping is a nicety but hardly a necessity on the networks you support.

However, if you are a networking professional working in computing environments that demand UTC accuracy and synchronization to within milliseconds, a solid grasp of NTP operations and redundancy techniques might prove to be your best friend. This book offers you the required tools to master the art and science of successful NTP deployment on networks of any size and supporting any type of business mission. This book also presents you with a multifaceted view of time and takes you on a journey through various historical periods that have played a role in shaping modern-day IT industry trends and NTP operations. Additionally, this book challenges NTP designers and developers to start planning for future NTP releases that incorporate relativistic and quantum components into it.

Who Should Read This Book?

Expert Network Time Protocol is aimed at the vast array of computing and networking professionals: network engineers, network infrastructure engineers, network administrators, network specialists, network designers, enterprise architects, and all who recognize that accurate and synchronized timekeeping is a critical element of modern-day computing and networking. This book is also aimed at anyone who at one time or another has grappled with time-related issues or has an interest in viewing time through different lenses. Additionally, this book is intended to stir the imagination of NTP designers and developers as they plan and deliberate future NTP releases.

How Is This Book Organized?

Expert Network Time Protocol consists of two parts: "NTP: The Key to Time Transcendence" and "NTP: The Story Behind the Accuracy and Synchronization of Network Time." The two parts are linked by a common theme: time. Chapters 1 and 2 comprise part 1, while part 2 is composed of Chapters 3, 4, and 5, the epilogue, the appendix, and the bibliography. The essence of each chapter follows:

Chapter 1, "Multiple Views of Time": Explore time from different perspectives: science, history, philosophy, and literature. Learn about the Julian and Gregorian calendars. Discover the timekeeping intricacies behind leap years that will prepare you for a discussion in Chapter 3 of how NTP accommodates leap seconds.

Chapter 2, "Network Administration and IT Trends Throughout History!": Navigate through key historical periods that helped shape modern-day IT industry trends and NTP operations.

Chapter 3, "NTP Operational, Historical, and Futuristic Overview": Learn about milestones in NTP development, reasons for NTP deployment, the Interplanetary Internet, and how the structure and content of NTP messages facilitate time synchronization.

Chapter 4, "NTP Architecture": Explore the complex nature of NTP deployment architecture as you delve into the nuts and bolts of NTP modes, sanity checks, security, and terminology.

Chapter 5, "NTP Design, Configuration, and Troubleshooting": Follow a four-step process to master the art and science of successful NTP deployment in multi-OS and multivendor networking environments of any size.

Epilogue, "NTP: A Journey in Time!": Share a moment of reflection with the author about writing the preceding pages.

Appendix, "Additional NTP Resources": Use the information provided about additional resources to continue expanding your knowledge on the subject of NTP.

Bibliography: Absorb yourself, as your time allows, in the thousands of pages of the publications that are referenced here to discover many more gems regarding the mysterious resource that this book is all about: time.

PART 1

∎∎∎

NTP: The Key to Time Transcendence

■ ■ ■

Multiple Views of Time

Sam smiled and pondered. His point of vantage offered him an unprecedented view and perspective. He wished they could catch even a glimpse of it. But his desire was tempered. How would they use it if they did? After all, so many of them misuse just about everything, let alone the power that this kind of knowledge and understanding could afford them.

And what of the apathy among them? So many no longer question the origin of the constant drumbeat of the circumstantial conveyer belts that submerge them continually in a multitude of exotic and mundane events. Instead, they simply accept that steady barrage either with mild content or, in many cases, with a sense of resignation. Sam was coming to grips with the realization that his audience might be limited because of so many of them being engaged in what appears to be a never-ending struggle with forces seemingly beyond their control. And for those interested, he would also have to be judicious in sharing his insights with them.

They, the humans, are occupying a wobbling, spherically shaped rock that follows what appears to be an elliptical orbit around Sam's native residence. Suffering from a collective amnesia, they've become bound by what they call *time* and confined to a minutest fraction of what they call *space*.

The legion of definitions of time that they've come up with only aids them in perpetuating this self-imposed ignorance of the time-transcendent laws that govern Sam's native habitat. They continually talk, write, and speculate about time. They keep track of it and attempt to "maximize" it. Their scientists have developed constructs called *calendars* and a stunning granularity of units to measure time's "passage." They identify some of it as *past* and some as *future* that's somehow divided by the elusive *present*.

As though it were a container of sorts, "their time" is filled with a host of routine and unexpected activities. They ascribe numerous attributes to those activities but have not yet grasped them as being nothing more than simple processes in energy conversion. They routinely try to find more time and use it as a resource to fuel the achievement of surprisingly meager goals. They repeatedly lament about being short of time as though capricious gods whimsically throttled its flow to them.

Yet, few among the humans give thought to transcending time. Somehow, they've become accustomed to its effects, even without understanding it. Their residence provides them with aids in perpetuating time's illusions. The inclination of Earth's axis to the plane in its orbital path creates an effect on the surface of their rock that they refer to as *seasons*. The change of seasons is a classic measure of time's "passage" for so many of them. Couple the effect of the seasons with their globe's rotation around its axis. The varying patterns of exposure of Earth's surface to the light rays from the sun create another means of time's illusory grip on their minds: the effects of *day* and *night*. With no awareness of ever having resided in the center of the sun where seasons, day, and night seem as most humorous concepts, they actually seem to enjoy time's numerous effects and ploys. And ploys they are indeed! Their obsession with aging, for one, being the biggest of them all!

Sam continued to muse. His earthly performances were drawing to a close. His smile broadened as he almost succumbed to sentimentality. He assumed many forms during his sojourn. Was it worth it? Or, better yet, using the familiar earthly vernacular, was it worth his time? His smile broadened even more.

He built. He fought. He prayed. He preached. The roles of a warrior, philosopher, gardener, priest, poet, housemaid, and scientist barely scratch the surface of his collective experience and confinement in the relativity of earthly time. All through those experiences Sam kept his wits about him. He murmured: yes, it was worth it! Through his efforts he has thinned the veil of time for some of them. He knew he wasn't quite finished, though. At least one more earthly adventure awaited him! And it seemed to be a timely one!

Sam was most conscious of his role as actor. He played all his parts with great zeal and dignity. After all, he volunteered for this job, and he loved it. Some of his roles were seductive, as though attempting to develop an identity of their own and distract him from his intended performance. He knew well how to guard against their pull, lest he forget his origins and become like the rest of them—lost in the earthly time. Occasionally, when his scripts appeared dim, he improvised. But hardly anyone around him ever noticed it.

In the course of acting out his many roles, Sam constantly marveled at the lack of a universal communication among the humans. The existence of myriad languages seemed a most primitive condition to him. They expend so much energy translating between the languages, but they don't seem to be able to agree on how to adopt a common one. Free will! he sighed. There will come a time when they will grasp its true meaning, he mused, while reminding himself to stop thinking in their limited terms.

Despite the many roles Sam played—all subject to the earthly time—his awareness had nothing to do with it. He acknowledged time as a meager construct to help him get through the numerous acts. A mere crutch! He had no sense of the beginning or ending of his roles. After all, all of his roles were all there, all at once. A most dynamic mosaic indeed! They differed from one another by the varying proportions of the different energy states from which they were composed and the dominant energy state they were last left in.

Sam's awareness pulsated with spectacular rhythm. Each of his earthly roles was an energy forcefield: all of the many "past" roles and the still remaining "future" one. At will, he could make any of the roles flash multidimensional imageries before him. They represented acts that he had already performed, a myriad of acts that could have been performed simply as a function of just the slightest variation of the conditions during the plays, and those acts that were still intended to play themselves out in the "future" role. Each role had numerous permutations regardless of its "past," "future," or "state of energy" condition.

Sam could make each role present itself exclusively in the form of sound, taking on qualities that would stun even the greatest of earthly musical connoisseurs. He could also view his roles via combinations of a seemingly endless spectrum of colors. He was able to access each role with ease and to any degree of detail he desired. It was a matter of acceleration, deceleration, and the application of the simplest of all energy conversion techniques, which despite its simplicity was still unknown to the humans. The technique that Sam used in a most natural and almost nonchalant manner has eluded the most sophisticated endeavors of their scientists, despite their continued quest for it.

Sam studied his many roles and assimilated their already played-out actualities and the seemingly limitless but unrealized possibilities. He found it relaxing and refreshing to switch between the different types of energy states in viewing the roles. Yet, he knew it was all prep, a rehearsal. No amount of study of any of his earthly roles could ultimately prepare him for the experience before him once the curtain was drawn upon his final act. He almost quivered with a degree of anticipation. Still, the prep was in order for his upcoming play, as he knew he was not quite finished.

As part of the preparation and rehearsal, Sam was able to access the collective essence of roles other than his own. He could view the numerous acts of many others like himself, as well as any particular condition or aspect of human knowledge, history, or experience that was of interest to him. He mused again. They've come a long way from what they call the prehistoric ages to the modern times. But what's blocking them from the realization of who they really are? He sighed. Time and space, what else?

Sam was able to function in many dimensions and move through them at will. One of his favorites, the "memory" dimension that he frequently visited, had a replica of all the content ever produced and recorded in any type of written, printed, graphic, audio, or video form by the earthlings. It was a replica native to that dimension, having naught to do with the bulkiness of the printed matter, the audio and video media, or even the clumsiness of their digitized counterparts. Not unlike Sam's many roles, the collective earthly content was a multistate energy forcefield. He could scan through it effortlessly, organize it, and sort it at will according to the most exotic criteria known by earthly standards.

The digitization of printed matter, voice, and images and the use of software they refer to as *search engines* were but crude approximations of his capabilities. In the "memory" dimension he scanned the combined achievements of earthly science, literature, philosophy, history, and more. He was most interested in the continuing evolution of their concept of time, their efforts at universal forms of communication through their modern computer networks, and their search for a unifying force behind what they call the four fundamental forces of nature: gravity, electromagnetism, and the strong and weak nuclear forces. In attempting to share any new insights with them, he knew he was facing an uphill struggle

given their collective attachments to their scientific method and theories, their philoso-
phies, their cultures, and their historical traditions.

Time: The Scientific Perspective

The science of physics that concerns itself with the study of matter/energy interactions
is governed by numerous laws and theories, most of which pertain to objects that are in
motion. The concept of motion, in turn, is irrevocably linked to that of time. Sam knew
he was entering a slippery slope. Objects, motion, time. To most of the earthlings these
concepts appear as very concrete, constant, and obvious. But their scientists have been
learning otherwise. The body of knowledge that constitutes physics has been punctuated
in the course of its expansion by numerous conflicts, contradictions, and inconsistencies,
in an effort to bring forth a clearer and more refined understanding of these fundamental
concepts.

Numerous laws and theories that have been advanced over the centuries of earthly
time flashed before Sam's awareness. They were all there, both silly and profound. Some
have been long discarded by a vast majority of the human race, others widely applied,
and still others hardly accepted or even understood. The dizzying display was almost
more than Sam cared to place his attention on: the laws of motion of classical mechanics,
electromagnetism, the special and general theory of relativity, quantum mechanics, Isaac
Newton's universal theory of gravitation, the string theory, and more. A multitude of the
finest of human minds have been involved in postulating and experimenting with these
laws, these theories, and the underlying mathematics behind them.

They all deal with the concepts of motion and time, from the micro to the macro
levels. From quarks to quasars, Sam murmured. And as much as they explain numerous
phenomena and provide a framework within which the humans can function, each new
theory seems to create its own set of seemingly irreconcilable conflicts with some of its
predecessor siblings, which only leads to the further pursuit of still newer theories and
explanations. As a whole, they only scratch the surface of the simple, elegant, and profound universal laws that Sam lived by.

With the predominance of their scientists adhering to the use of the scientific method
in advancing their knowledge of universal laws, it will take a major paradigm shift for
them to break out of this ever-increasing but ever more confining scientific box. Will they
recognize how to break out of it? Would they accept it if someone told them how to do it?
Or, do they have to discover the escape hatch for themselves through seemingly endless
trial and error?

Sam mused. The inherent reliance of the scientific method on the process of experi-
mentation to prove a hypothesis is ultimately a trap. It confines all of their experiments
that are aimed at a better understanding of time, space, and the structure of matter to a
limited number of dimensions and energy states—those in which their experimental

instruments can function. A pity indeed! They've become conditioned to trust inanimate objects more than themselves. They truly do not know who they really are!

In all cases, the instruments they use in conducting their experiments seem to interfere with the results of those experiments, no matter how minute and, in most instances, irrelevant the interference might be in the context of "everyday life." But that interference makes itself known and becomes much more pronounced at the subatomic level, which is where they seem to be continually baffled by new discoveries and phenomena. They've even come up with a principle to reflect the limitation in their ability to determine with absolute precision the state of the particles that constitute their very forms: the "uncertainty principle."

The knowledge they continue to gain via the scientific method creates a box, one that perhaps grows bigger as a function of their time but never transcends its fundamental nature. Is anyone among them willing to abandon some of the elements of the scientific method in pursuit of a still more refined understanding of time? What are the consequences in the face of such audacity given the seemingly profound accomplishments the scientific method has afforded them so far?

Classical Mechanics

Most of the earthly activities that are perceptible to the human senses fit neatly into the laws of classical mechanics where the motion of objects is very, very slow compared to the speed of light and objects are much, much bigger than the subatomic particles—or even the largest atoms—from which they are composed. Inasmuch as the earthly scientists seem to have adopted the speed of light as a universal constant (approximately 299,792.5 km/sec or 186,282 miles/sec using the commonly accepted ratio of 1.609344 km/mile or 0.621371 miles/km), the absolutely exact speed of light is still unknown and subject to experimental error.

The most common approximations for the speed of light are stated either as 300,000 km/sec or as 186,000 miles/sec. Close enough, Sam murmured, especially when comparing the typical speeds of the common earthly objects to the speed of light. After all, the speed of 186,000 miles/sec is roughly ten million times that of a car traveling at 67 miles/hr. But, in the final analysis, Sam muttered, they really don't know much of anything with absolute precision. Everything they do and measure is an approximation, subject to uncertainty and error, even though each of their acts could be perceived with an immutable reality and precision even from the slowest pulsating dimensions in which he resides.

Despite the fact that classical mechanics breaks down and becomes completely inadequate at speeds approaching the speed of light, Newton's laws of motion still serve the earthlings quite well. In the course of the application of those laws, most of them make an inherent assumption that all time-related measurements happen in a coordinate system or a frame of reference that is at rest. The size of their wobbly rock, no matter how minute from Sam's perspective, seems to offer them this comfort of immutability and absoluteness. And it is, indeed, a fairly safe bet for many of their routine activities,

Sam thought. It's a given that while driving a car, configuring Network Time Protocol (NTP) on a router, or diving into a pool, not too many (if any) give thought to the rate of motion of their solar system through the Milky Way galaxy, the rate of motion of their galaxy with respect to other galaxies, or even the rate of motion of their own wobbly rock around the sun.

Just ask any of them: how fast were you traveling between A to B, where A and B represent locations on your rock? Not too many will factor in the approximately 18.5 miles/sec orbital speed of their rock around the sun when giving an answer. Otherwise, the answer might be, "During the last hour, I traveled at approximately 45 miles/hr between A and B, but I also traveled approximately 66,585 miles around the sun." Not the most likely answer!

Sam smiled again. He knew how time is intertwined in every aspect of their lives and how their daily activities are structured around the various units of time. He could not help but wonder how many could define the base unit of earthly time, which is a second. How many would be able to define a second in terms other than as a portion of a still larger unit (a minute, an hour, or a day) or movement of one of the arms on a clock, the instrument that tracks time.

Definition of an Atomic Second

Webster's dictionary defines a *second*, or the base unit of time in the International System of Units, as being "equal to the duration of 9,192,631,770 periods of the radiation corresponding to the transition between the two hyperfine levels of the ground state of the cesium-133 atom."

A definition of *duration* is "the time during which something exists or lasts."

One of the definitions of *period* is "the interval of time required for a cyclic motion or phenomenon to complete a cycle and begin to repeat itself."

Sam tried not to laugh. They define time with time! He empathized, though, with their plight. It's almost impossible to define time when you are confined by it and can't look outside of it. Their systems of transportation and all manner of commerce rely on time, or at least a system for "measuring" it. They get paid for performing services based on some units of time. He sighed as with mild resignation.

They don't really have to understand time to navigate through it and take advantage of some of its seemingly beneficial, however transient, effects. But without fully understanding time, they are also subject to all of its impersonal ills. They simply have not grasped time as a form of energy itself that facilitates transformations between other energy forms—an interface of sorts! They should be able to relate to the concept of an interface! At least their scientists have acknowledged time as another dimension, which is a step in the right direction!

And because time is used in defining speed (including the speed of light!), it is a component of one of the most renowned equations that specifies energy/matter equivalence. But what if they did grasp time as another form of energy? Would that motivate them to transcend it? They would have to be given a vision of the possibilities resulting from the transcendence of time! Otherwise, given their propensities to discuss, analyze, and argue about everything, they would probably get stuck on the issue of why they should choose some forms of energy as preferable over others for their habitation. Sam sighed again.

Definition of a Clock

Sam knew what was still before him in one of his yet-to-be-played-out acts. He also knew why his role was critical. Most network administrators consider the configuration of the current NTP as a trivial and boring task. After all, it's just a matter of clock synchronization between devices. There are plenty of far more exciting and complex protocols to configure. NTP and its configuration are passé, they think.

The protocol alphabet soup flashed before him. He could see how NTP paled in the eyes of net admins as compared to the nuances of BGP, MPLS, or even the commonly used NAT. However, those who trivialize NTP deal with network components that are stationary with respect to each other and their commonly (almost unconsciously) used frame of reference, their wobbling planet. From the standpoint of physics they are still in the age of classical mechanics. But they can't stay in that frame of mind and at that level of NTP functionality and configuration forever!

They should recognize by now that classical mechanics works only for a limited range of speeds and object sizes. Large-scale space exploration and migrations to other solar systems at speeds approaching that of light (and beyond!) are looming and gaining ground. Then there is the miniaturization of networking components to subatomic levels. They will need to get a grip on relativistic and quantum components of NTP sooner or later.

Sam continued to rehearse the possibilities during his "future" role. The lack of NTP synchronization could ultimately shatter their interstellar travel plans through time-related miscommunications. They have not yet faced the challenge of galactic and intergalactic hackers attempting to disrupt their entire communications infrastructure and commerce that depend so much on synchronized and correct time, he grumbled. Their effort to grasp what's beyond their wobbling rock could be completely undermined! And even the Internet, as they know it now, could collapse because of flooding with bogus time information.

But to address the issues of a "future" robust NTP and the Internet extending its reach through at least a portion of their galaxy, they will have to grasp how to transmit information at speeds greater than even the speed of light, Sam mused. In the contest between Newton and Albert Einstein, it seemed for a while that Newton's theory of gravity could have been the answer to transcending the speed of light. Newton's theory of gravity implied that the transmission of gravitational influences between objects was instantaneous regardless of the distance between them. But the formidable Einstein seems to have prevailed in that contest. His general theory of relativity, which deals with gravity and accelerated motion, still affirms the invariance of the speed of light. Since Einstein defined a new frontier, he may have to lead the way to transcend it, Sam continued to muse.

If the humans plan to do any serious communication over long spatial distances, they will eventually have to revisit the idea of an information transmission vehicle operating at speeds greater than that of light, whether that vehicle be a new and revised understanding of the nature of the gravitational field or perhaps the yet-to-be-discovered means of time transcendence. Else, they may be waiting for long periods of time between their transmissions and receptions. When it comes to understanding the fundamental forces of nature, he thought, they still see only the individual fingers of a hand protruding from behind an unknown veil. They don't yet perceive the hand.

Sam stepped back for a moment from the possibilities of his future "role" and turned his attention to a core NTP concept, that of clocks, the keepers of earthly time. Webster's definitions again flashed before him. "A device other than a watch for indicating or measuring time…" or "any periodic system by which time is measured." Their concept of clocks will require a revolution of its own, he concluded.

The Special Theory of Relativity

It has been a century in terms of the earthly time since the special theory of relativity was proposed. The concept of time among the earth's physicists and scientists has not been the same since. And it has been a solid step forward in recognizing the true nature of time. However, Sam's fundamental challenge of bringing to their attention the need for transcending time has not changed. What portion out of the total population really cares about the change in the concept of time that took place in that memorable year of 1905 as measured by some of their calendars? he wondered. Surrounded and saturated by phenomena where the effects of the theory of relativity are beyond detection by their physical senses, they continue to embrace the concreteness and invariance of time. What creatures of habit!

In resolving the paradox stemming from Newton's laws of motion and Maxwell's laws of electromagnetism, the special theory of relativity overturned the concept of the invariance of time and replaced it with the assumption about the invariance of the speed of light. The theory concludes that

- The experience of time appears to vary as a function of one's motion relative to a frame of reference.

- The concept of motion becomes meaningless, unless it is defined with respect to, or as being relative to, another object.

Yet, the principle of relative motion does not apply to light itself, which appears to travel at a constant speed regardless of an observer's frame of reference.

According to the special theory of relativity, clocks and/or objects such as humans, NTP servers, space vehicles, or subatomic particles that are moving at the highest speeds with respect to a stationary frame of reference (that's if you can really find one!) appear to experience the greatest "time dilation" from the perspective of observers who are located in that frame of reference. This means time appears to move slowest for those who are observed moving at the highest speed and, vice versa, fastest for those at rest. The time dilation factor, which is derived from Hendrik Lorentz's transformation equations, is equivalent to the square root of the difference between 1 and the square of the object's velocity divided by the square of the speed of light, Sam thoughtfully observed.

Since those who are at rest with respect to a frame of reference appear to experience time at its "normal" or fastest rate, the experience of time by a network administrator on board a space station ferrying an NTP stratum 1 reference clock into the vastness of outer space should vary from that of his or her compatriot observing the space vehicle from the safe and secure surroundings of an earthly lab.

Sam did not have to be convinced that without a relativistic NTP, the earthbound administrators might experience time-related problems in their attempts to maintain NTP synchronization with the distant fast-moving space vehicles and satellites. His current point of vantage offered him that perspective already, even without delving into their theories. But even that wasn't quite it for NTP. To escape the planetary gravity and to reach higher and higher speeds, the spacecraft was not going to move at a constant speed with respect to the lab. It was going to be subject to acceleration from its own power sources as well as gravitational influences from far and wide across the galaxy and beyond. Incorporating the impact of the special theory of relativity into NTP was a good start. But more was required.

The special theory of relativity is called "special" for a reason. What makes it "special" is the absence of the consideration of the force of gravity and accelerated motion. The special theory of relativity deals only with constant velocities or nonaccelerated, uniform motions. While providing an initial framework for the breaking of the mold of time, NTP configurations will eventually have to account for clocks traveling at varying speeds and subject to gravitation's influences, which is the domain of general relativity.

The General Theory of Relativity

According to the mass/energy equivalence principle stemming from special relativity, if the increasing mass of a clock did not require increasing amounts of energy to keep accelerating it toward the speed of light, the clock could possibly reach a point where its time would stand still from the perspective of outside observers; i.e., the clock would have reached the speed of light, which today's world of science accepts as an impossibility.

Having clocks made from light itself might certainly satisfy the desires of many who are dismayed at the seemingly swift passage of time in their lives! No doubt there is an element of transcendence here, Sam pondered. But they have not grasped how to reach that transcendence except through experimentations that try to approximate it at the subatomic levels. At least they are trying!

If light itself could be used to construct an NTP clock—light that already moves at the speed of light—then that clock could become the ultimate NTP clock source. After all, that clock would not experience the passage of time at all! That could be the ultimate synchro-nization on the interplanetary and interstellar Internet. The question is, are they ready for it? What would they do if suddenly they found themselves without the crutch of time, as they know it?

Sam scanned the "role" known as Einstein, who grappled with the issue of time for almost the entire duration of his earthly act. Overturning the concreteness of the con-cept of time with special relativity—which elegantly allows for the dilation of time—he faced even a bigger challenge before him: something out there apparently moves faster than even the speed of light, in direct defiance of what he just came up with. It's the gravitational influences between objects. The one who played Newton smiled at Ein-stein's dilemma. Temporarily absent from the earthly stage, he cheered Einstein on from behind the scenes.

Newton's theory of gravity was standing fast to the test of time, even as Einstein struggled with its continued blatant challenge to his newly proclaimed invariant icon, the speed of light. His torment, frustration, and insight produced a warp in time and space. The space warps explain how gravitational influences between objects are trans-mitted, but they also cap the speed of those transmissions to the speed of light. The time warps, in turn, explain how clocks slow down in the presence of strong gravitational fields. Newton relaxed from behind the scenes even though his theory of gravity did not survive its greatest challenge: Einstein's mind. But Einstein was a worthy competitor, and Newton did not mind the general theory of relativity transcending his theory of gravity. He also knew that the two of them still had a common mission together: transcendent NTP. Einstein was also pleased. The special and general theories were now one theory of relativity, in harmony with gravity. A potentially deadly conflict was solved. But as both players anticipated, a new one was born.

As an actor in a complex planetary energy state, Einstein was a team player. But he could not have anticipated the impact that his theories would have on NTP. He planned a break from science and a "future" role as a poet. Sam empathized. The Einstein-turned-poet would read about NTP breakthroughs and praise them through his relativistic poetry, Sam chuckled.

But even as Einstein anticipated a poet's role in a drastically different planetary energy state, he was gradually becoming aware of the quantum foam that was enveloping him and his theories. Many of his fellow players were more and more becoming aware of the sub-atomic chaos. Einstein was glad he was planning a poet's role. The resolution of conflict that would arise between general relativity and the quantum world was somebody else's job. And so was quantum NTP, Sam remarked.

Quantum Mechanics

Considering the spectrum of current human scientific frontiers—from micro to macro—Sam observed that the quantum world comes closest to breaking down the concreteness of human thinking regarding time, space, and the properties of objects. Not without a reason! he grinned. The laws of classical mechanics that govern how an object behaves seem to be clearly differentiated from the object's properties that define what an object is. But that's not the case at the quantum level. At the quantum level, the properties of an "object" (typically, a subatomic particle) can become indistinguishable from the "object's" behavior. An NTP server viewed from a quantum perspective is simply not the bulk and concrete-like solid matter that it appears to be to the human senses. Its very existence is a matter of probability, rather than certainty.

While the human senses function in the range of speeds, frequencies, and distances that produce seemingly meaningful results according to classical physics, Sam knew that this condition was not going to continue forever—borrowing from their own terminology. The yet-unperceived (not played out according to their senses) planetary energy states—where not only the laws of quantum and relativistic behavior but also those of transcendence routinely prevail over the classics—were but a matter of their "time." Those states will demand a quantum and relativistic approach to NTP configuration and time synchronization. Else…. He chose, for now, not to focus on the consequences of the current NTP being deployed in the planetary energy states dominated by quantum and relativity principles. From prior scans, he knew they could be ugly.

Sam flashed before him the roles of the players who would participate in the "future" effort to incorporate quantum and relativistic principles into NTP. He worked with some of them in his "past" roles. He smiled as he reviewed their interactions. Some of them take themselves entirely too seriously, without recognizing they are just playing a part, he thought. They want to call themselves "inventors" just because they happen to be the first humans to stumble across something that already exists and is well understood in other dimensions. Human labels, he sighed. They need to spend more time in the center of the sun, he quipped. Labels dissolve there fast!

While the "future" NTP developers were going about their earthly business in their current roles, they were unaware of Sam's scientific and historical searches within the memory dimension. His NTP explorations escaped them as well. But they all shared a common bond without even being fully conscious of it. Sam detected that they all had a sense of the protocol's incompleteness. This bond would draw them together in an upcoming planetary energy state where quantum and relativistic principles would come into their own. Sam was aware, however, that the quantum and relativistic components would still be insufficient to bring NTP to completeness. The NTP transcendence component was ultimately inevitable.

In comparison with the special theory of relativity, whose effects become pronounced at very high speeds (by human standards, that is!), quantum mechanics operate at the subatomic levels where the distances are extremely small and durations of events tend to be extremely short (again, by human standards!). But human perceptions, even if propped up by the most accurate of instruments, are relative at best.

For those particles whose "visits" into the quantum world result from collisions and interactions with other particles, the fact that they spend a billionth or less of a human second in the quantum world does not diminish an "entire lifetime" experience for them. Try telling this to the earthlings, Sam grumbled with frustration that in a fraction of their second they could experience a lifetime and more in dimensions to which they are connected by an energy form that they have not yet grasped or been able to measure! Convincing them that NTP will need a quantum component will be a sufficient challenge, let alone that there is an entirely new form of energy that defies the very best of their science.

If more of them took a closer look at the quantum theory, the idea of an invisible and immeasurable energy force might not appear so strange to them. After all, what is the source of energy that powers the motion of the electron clouds in orbit around the atoms' nuclei? Is this not an example of a perpetual motion machine that defies human attempts to invent one at the level of classical physics because of the conservation laws?

Sam flashed a simple scenario before him of a ceiling fan. The blades are discrete when they are not in motion. Their position is clearly observable by the human senses. Turn the fan on at high speed. It's a matter of a flip of a switch. Suddenly, the human senses perceive a whirling circle and lose sight of the individual blades. Commonsense human experience dictates that you don't stick your hand into that circle. A hospital visit might otherwise follow! To an observer from another world who is totally unfamiliar with house construction and the operation of electricity on the planet, the moving fan might appear as a perpetual motion machine. After all, seemingly it goes on, and on, and on. The observer might not be there long enough to view the action of turning the fan on and off. Unaware of the energy that's being supplied to the fan via the invisible electric wiring, the otherworldly observer might sit in awe of a moving ceiling fan.

Sam flashed back to the quantum world. They have the examples before them, visible to the senses even in their everyday life, he thought. What do they need to recognize the electrons' connection to other dimensions and by inference their own connection as well? Do they want such recognition? What would they do with it? He refocused on NTP. He knew it was the key.

Sam probed the reaction of a network administrator whose NTP server suddenly began to behave according to the laws of quantum mechanics. "Now you see it, now you don't. Now it's here, now it's not," he mused. With no certainties and only probabilities in the net admin's arsenal, Sam envisioned the administrator applying for a job and answering a question regarding NTP configuration during an interview. With an answer like "Now you see, now you don't. Now it's here, now it's not," the net admin might have a hard time finding a job in the world that's dominated by the worship of classical networking!

The Superstring Theory

Both the quantum theory and the general theory of relativity seemingly operate at the opposite outer edges of everyday human experience. The quantum theory governs the apparent chaos of very small "objects"—some having extremely brief lives—that are operating at very short distances in the subatomic world. As Sam scanned the status of network administration across the planet, he was quite aware that only a few network administrators at the "present time" are at all concerned about the impact of quantum phenomena on their networks and specifically on NTP configuration. He was satisfied, however, that at least a few popped up in his scan.

As contrasted to the quantum theory, the general theory of relativity, with its time and space warps to account for gravitational influences, is most pronounced when dealing with very large objects (planets, stars, galaxies, and more) that are usually separated by very large distances. How large those distances really are remains to be seen, given the warping of time and space, Sam murmured.

The happy medium of classical physics with its concreteness of time and space seems to offer a great deal of comfort and stability to the lives of the earthly inhabitants and the network administrators among them. It hides from the day-to-day activities the apparent conflict between the two giants that are operating at the opposite ends of modern-day science. But are those ends really opposite? He went on to scan the level of concern for the effect of general relativity on computer networks, time synchronization, and NTP configuration. There was little concern, he concluded. But some concern was beginning to percolate, even if peripherally.

Sam zeroed in on a planetary energy state yet to be outplayed. The conflict between the quantum theory and the general theory of relativity was gone. The nature of the perpetual motion machines of the subatomic world was clearly understood, not questioned. The long quest for unification of what they now perceive as the four fundamental forces of nature was over. The actions of gravity were at last understood, but only after they were able to view them from dimensions not subject to gravitational influences. The computer networks that spanned a corner of their galaxy hardly resembled the bulkiness of the current hardware and the lack of sophistication of the current protocols. Remarkable progress, he thought.

As Sam accurately observed, NTP with its relativistic, quantum, and transcendent components was a major force for change in reaching that state. Numerous players had contributed through many acts, during what seemed a long time by earthly standards. Sam noted the confusion and argumentation that reigned along the way. But there is the potential to pull it off, he thought, especially with those who portrayed the roles of Einstein and Newton leading the way. After a few poetic breaks, that is! But Sam also knew the difference between the played-out and the yet-unplayed planetary energy states. They will have to operate at the blueprint frequency of their roles—or very close to it—in order to directly experience that state. He was nonetheless hopeful. His experience of that state was independent of theirs.

Sam's attention shifted to the relentless quest for a deeper understanding of time, space, and the world in which they live. New theories were emerging in their thinking. The big problem, however, was the continued reliance on experiments with instruments that were increasingly interfering with the experiments' outcomes in order to prove the theories.

The string theory remains elegant in spite of all of the ups and downs it has experienced since their scientists began toying with the idea of tiny strings composing all matter. There is elegance in the supersymmetry theories as well. There is elegance in combining them into a superstring theory. There is elegance in the concept of innumerable tiny strings vibrating to create the appearance of a quark, an electron, or a neutron start. But the very concept of vibration is again irrevocably linked with that of time. Thus, Sam continued to observe that even the increased understanding of the structure of matter and the potential resolution of conflict between quantum mechanics and general relativity have not freed them from the confining ravages of time. At least with the superstring theory, they are openly talking about other dimensions! Perhaps as doorways for transcending time! This is what some of their philosophers and poets have done for centuries! he thought.

Time: The Philosophical Perspective

Ah, philosophy. Sam flashed before him the numerous definitions from Webster's dictionary: "a discipline comprising at its core logic, aesthetics, ethics, metaphysics, and epistemology"; "a search for a general understanding of values and reality by chiefly speculative rather than observational means"; and "the most general beliefs, concepts and attitudes of an individual or a group." There were more.

Philosophy was another means of expressing their quest or thirst for the understanding of who they are, he thought. While philosophy gives them considerable license in expressing themselves, it also implies that each individual or group could have its own concept of time. He was neither concerned nor totally surprised by it. He continued with the results of his scan for their understanding of time from a philosophical perspective.

Next he flashed the references to time from the *Concise Routledge Encyclopedia of Philosophy*. Not much help here: "Time is the single most pervasive component of our experience and the most fundamental concept in our physical theories." Sam already explored the scientific perception of time in physical theories. And the "pervasive component of our experience" sounds like a nice substitute for "past," "present," and "future." This is a clever way to define and describe something that's not understood, he sighed.

Sam did another pass and brought forth the definition of time from one of their prestigious philosophical publications: *The Cambridge Dictionary of Philosophy*. No surprises here either. There were several quotes of their foremost philosophers defining time in circular terms through the use of temporal notions and then an admission that "time may be too basic to admit a definition."

Given the lack of agreement on what time is, it's small wonder that they can so readily accept its effects, continually measure it as though they know exactly what it is, and occasionally even agree on what time it is. Sam admired the spirit of quest, though. They've got it in them to transcend it. They've found the boundaries. Now, can they go beyond them?

Time: The Historical Perspective

Sam thought for a moment. How does one explain to them the processes of energy conversion that their earthly habitat and they themselves participate in, without subjecting those processes to the confines of earthly time? Epochs, eras, calendars, and a variety of time units are nothing more but an attempt to identify and place labels on the collective planetary energy states. The crutch of time allows them to view the changes in these states as a sort of growth or evolution, a comfortable progression in time.

Sam was absorbed in the results of his historical scan of the billions of inhabitants of the human race. Each human is an energy source, although most are unaware of it. Each plays numerous roles, and each role has countless energy state possibilities. The optimal energy state represents a role's blueprint. Sam knew the potential was there for each of the billions of roles to resonate at their "blueprint" frequency. He focused on it. It was a transcendent experience!

The spectrum of colors, music, and multidimensional shapes were all pulsating in a harmonious self-transcending and energy-creating state. But what were the odds against them reaching that state? Enormous! He recalled the seductive nature of some of his own roles. Is it a wonder they've become quite cynical about a perpetual motion machine, a fountain of youth, or nonpolluting, self-sustaining, and regenerative energy sources? His preceding scientific explorations into the "future" of NTP kept him hopeful, though.

The potential to achieve the blueprint conditions by the humans was there, despite those conditions having been relegated by the greatest of their thinkers to the realm of unattainable ideals and even as being contrary to the laws of nature. But the many non-blueprint states of the billions of roles exerted an enormously dampening influence on each one of them. It would require an unparalleled degree of synchronization on their part to reach out for that unique collective state. However, given their obsession with time and ever more robust computer networks, Sam continued to be hopeful. The synchronization of their computing devices via NTP was, in fact, the first step, he surmised. It was a precursor to, and a chance to practice at, achieving of an energy state that has not yet occurred throughout their history.

So that's what they call *history*! Sam exclaimed. "A chronological record of significant events (as affecting a nation or institution) often including an explanation of their causes." He was grateful for the Webster "role." He verified *chronological*. It's "of, relating to, or arranged in or according to the order of time" or "reckoned in units of time." But without the ability to navigate in the memory dimension where the energy states of the planet and all of its inhabitants are recorded with unerring precision, their history represents a very deformed and an incomplete description of an interplay between the billions of roles and the energy states of their planet, he concluded.

He focused on another reference to time in *The Life of Greece* from the Story of Civilization series, by Will Durant, who wrote, "Civilizations are always older than we think, and under whatever sod we tread are the bones of men and women who also worked and loved, wrote songs and made beautiful things, but whose names and being have been lost in the careless flow of time."

Sam saw how a statement like this could come from the confines of earthly time. But even from the perspective of their limited understanding of the law of conservation of energy, the roles of earthly inhabitants are never lost. Energy conversion is not a loss. Inaccessibility or the inability to navigate the memory dimension is not a loss. It has become a convenient means of accepting the bondage of time. And the component of each role that extends into other dimensions and acts as its own energy source defies not just the concept of loss in time but the very principle of conservation of energy, which appears relevant only in the relativity of earthly time.

The Calendars

As a means of imposing their own sense of organization upon the interplay of their earthly roles and planetary energy states, humans have come up with the concept of calendars. The calendar construct affords the longer units of time (days, weeks, months, years) some semblance of order. The many types of calendars that have been developed and used throughout human history attest to the imperfection and lack of precision of this construct. Yet, the calendar's usefulness is seemingly undeniable in most of their activities.

The Julian Calendar

Sam zeroed in on the planetary energy state, which from the current human perspective of the 21st century AD is viewed as the year 46 BC. For a moment, he skipped the controversy surrounding the religious connotations associated with the BC (Before Christ) and the AD (Anno Domini) abbreviations in referencing time. CE (Common Era) and BCE (Before Common Era) are nothing more than a set of labels replacing AD and BC for the convenience of those whose sensibilities were being offended by even an approximation of religious reference in timekeeping. Humans, he sighed. Don't they have anything better to do with their time than argue about labels?

He zoomed in on the state of affairs in Rome. He took note of Julius Caesar making an observation about the lack of synchronization of the widely used Roman calendar with the earthly seasons. Anticipating a planetary energy state where the synchronization between network devices—and not just with planetary seasons—becomes a matter of life and death in the "future" wars that he was still to fight, Caesar decided to commission an Alexandrian Greek, Sosigenes, to bring order to the Roman method of keeping track of time. Sosigenes complied, and the Julian calendar was born.

Although Marcus Tullius Cicero, a Roman statesman, orator, and essayists, quips that Caesar is not satisfied with simply ruling the earth but rather feels compelled to regulate the stars as well, the Roman Senate accepts Caesar's calendar reform. Days are added to the then-current year, the duration of months is changed, and, however still imperfect and imprecise, the Julian calendar begins to take hold throughout the civilized world. Somehow, Caesar sensed he had "future" roles to play where a more precise tracking of time would be a key to his success. Sam was quite amused by the calendar restructuring activities in 46 BC.

The Julian calendar introduced two varying duration years—the more common 365-day year and the rarer 366-day leap year—with the fundamental building block of the calendar being a combination of the three "common" years followed by a single leap year. Someone also had to be responsible for imposing the correct sequence of the "common" and leap years upon the time-conscious public throughout the empire.

But the Roman timekeepers entrusted with the task of calendar administration made a mistake, a costly one that almost tripped Caesar in his "future" acts. They altered the fundamental building block of the Julian calendar to consist of two "common" years and one leap year instead of three and one, respectively. It took them some time to discover the error, with historians placing the discovery at around 9 BC, as viewed through the most commonly accepted and used calendar of the modern times.

By the time 9 BC rolled around, the years 45 BC, 42 BC, 39 BC, 36 BC, 33 BC, 30 BC, 27 BC, 24 BC, 21 BC, 18 BC, 15 BC, 12 BC, and 9 BC were already "past" and classified as leap years. The remedy, however, proved to be amazingly simple. Skip the leap years for a few "future" cycles to compensate for the error. The addition of leap years resumed in AD 8, leaving a 17-year period without a leap year. Sam decided to skip the review of the Roman public's reaction to the calendar adjustments. Needless to say, it was a turbulent time.

Sam mused. The humans are only concerned with time synchronization moving forward into the "future." But their clocks could be equally well synchronized to tick into the "past." The many time-related mysteries haunting their historians could easily be solved. For that to happen, they must be ready for another revolutionary change in their understanding of time. The special theory of relativity was a decent start in undoing the notion of time's concreteness. However, they must begin to get used to the idea of total transcendence of time.

Sam continued with the calendar scan. The use of the Julian calendar outlived the fall of the Western Roman Empire by more than 1,000 years, but in the year AD 1582, the Julian calendar gave way to its more modern successor, the Gregorian calendar.

The Gregorian Calendar

By the time the planetary energy state of AD 1582 was reached, the effects of the inaccuracies in the Julian calendar were becoming pronounced in terms of lack of synchronicity with the earthly seasons. The average Julian year (four consecutive years that would include a leap year divided by four) was simply a little bit longer than one complete trip of the planet around the sun, which is what a calendar was supposed to reflect. The effects of the Julian calendar inaccuracies were not unlike the effects of the inaccuracies of the Roman calendar prior to Caesar's decision to reform it.

In AD 1582, the role of Caesar was not around to initiate another calendar reform, even though Caesar had other performances since that fateful day of the "ides of March," 44 BC. It was on that day when one of his closest friends and a co-conspirator against him, Decimus Brutus, convinced him to come to the Senate floor, only to reach a dramatic conclusion of his role through the knives of the assassins. None of the roles he played since that day rose to the occasion of another calendar reform, although as a dedicated actor he was becoming increasingly aware of the growing discrepancies in keeping track of time resulting from his own reform.

In AD 1582, the figure of authority in the parts of the world where the Roman Empire had once flourished was Pope Gregory the XIII. It took the pope's decree to advance the calendar forward by ten days to compensate for the seemingly imperceptible discrepancies that were gradually introduced by the Julian calendar over the past 1,600+ years. Not everyone present on the stage of 1582 was thrilled about the Gregorian calendar reform. Some reckoned, quite correctly, that the due dates for their accounts payable were being unfairly accelerated!

Without a global computer network to flash instantaneously the pope's decision around the world, it took decades and even centuries of earthly time for some of the countries to switch their timekeeping practices to the new Gregorian calendar. And the introduction of the Gregorian calendar did not equate with the elimination of the Julian calendar. Thus, with the Julian, Gregorian, and other calendars in operation in varying parts of the world, the growing confusion regarding timekeeping was simply a matter of time! Yet, as Sam accurately noted, while becoming more aware of the need to "measure" time with greater synchronicity to the earthly seasons, humans still did not understand what time was, even as they incessantly continued to observe its apparent effects based on their planet's journey around its native star.

Sam grinned. The changing mass of the earth and the sun will not keep the planet Earth in the same identical orbit time after time. There simply are no two identical energy states within the solar system, no matter how repetitive its operation seems to their senses and instruments. Just as the effects of the special theory of relativity may be imperceptible to their senses and instruments under "typical and normal" conditions, the changing mass of their habitat and their main energy source—as they know it in the limited three dimensions—will eventually become a factor in measuring time. Add to this the gravitational effects of the remaining planets and all manner of space debris populating the solar system. Not one trip around the sun is the same. Not one of their years is the same. What will it take for them to receive a true understanding of time?

NTP flashed before him again. Ultimately, the only hope for their computer networks to sustain the apparent ravages of time is to incorporate a component into NTP, an algorithm that considers time for what it is, an energy source, not an effect of the changing energy states.

Other Earthly Calendars

As a result of his historical scan, Sam was aware of other calendar constructs. The details of the Mayan, Babylonian, Hindu, Iranian, Chinese, and Aztec calendars flashed before him. There were others. Some calendars were still unknown to their modern-day scientists and historians. The Atlanteans, for one, were very adept at keeping track of time, exceeding even the modern-day methodologies. They also came close to grasping time as an energy source.

In the Atlantean measurements of the earth's orbital path around the sun, there was not the slightest gravitational influence originating either from the farther reaches of the universe or from within the solar system itself that went undetected. Their ability to calibrate time with absolute precision to the special relationship between the sun and the earth was a marvel that would astound even the greatest of their modern-day astronomers. But, not unlike other time trackers still before them, they, too, reveled greatly in their apparent mastery of measuring time without making a collective effort to transcend it. Eventually, they found themselves subject to time's apparent ravages. Sam marveled: all those attempts at keeping track of time, all those failures to transcend it. How long will this energy source last for them?

In each civilization that created its own calendar, the use of NTP was a distant anticipation but not a played-out energy state. Up until now, the apparent lack of effort to manifest the blueprint energy state by the numerous roles, effectively, prevented NTP from becoming a more developed instrument for transcending time. Sam knew that not unlike the myriad of languages that require a phenomenal expenditure of energy to translate between them, the use of NTP in ultimately transcending time could succeed only when a singular and universal means of keeping track of time was adapted. He was pleased those efforts were well underway.

If they grasp the clues that are offered them by the synchronization of their computer networks, then there is the potential they can make a leap and discover the synchronization of their internal clocks. Else, he mused, it's probably again a matter of time before the energy state that buried the Atlanteans buries them again. He preferred not to contemplate that energy state possibility.

Given the various energy states to which the humans refer to as *catastrophes*—that occur so often as a result of miscommunication between them regarding time—Sam zeroed in on their current synchronization mechanisms. He wanted to be perfectly clear about them in order to minimize any potential for a catastrophe during his upcoming role. He knew that catastrophes usually require a cleanup. He wasn't sure if he wanted to play a subsequent, additional cleanup role.

There are quite a few time synchronization tools, he murmured: time zones, daylight savings, standard, leap year, and more. Some are intended to provide an approximate measure of constancy between the daylight hours and the direct exposure of Earth's surface to the sun. The current planetary energy state prevented the simultaneous exposure of the entire surface to the rays from the sun. A temporary measure, indeed! They ultimately have the power to change it! For now, it's a condition that aids them in perpetuating their sense of time.

Leap Year: The Earthly Time Synchronizer

The simplicity of a leap year is appealing. It's a year in which an extra day is added to the calendar in order to synchronize it with the earthly seasons. However, for a leap year to be even somewhat effective, the calendar in question needs to approximate the duration of one earthly trip around the sun.

Before the idea of the leap year came along and the Greek Sosigenes incorporated it into the Julian calendar, synchronization of the seasons with the calendars of the time occurred via the addition of varying number of days to the different calendars of the times. Revelry, festivities, and celebrations often marked the "extra" days. Effectively, time stood still from the calendar perspective but not necessarily so from the perspective of creditors and debtors. Paying bills on time could have been very tricky in those days!

Sam wondered how modern-day network administrators would have handled NTP synchronization during such times. It's better that some avoided the experience even as they well understood that all were role-playing during different planetary energy states. The memory of a role during which they were asked to fight a lion with their bare hands in a Roman arena for the sin of inaccurate NTP synchronization could have prevented those actors from taking on the net admin roles in modern times!

Even as the idea of a leap year is very appealing, it is not without its faults. The energy states of the solar system that incorporate the spatial relationship between the earth and the sun have defied earthly scientists and astronomers throughout human history to identify them with absolute precision. Incorporating a leap year to the Julian calendar was a good first step, but doing so with regularity every four years eventually led to a significant offset between the seasons and the calendar and played a role in giving birth to the Gregorian calendar.

The addition of a leap year into the Gregorian calendar seems a bit more sophisticated than the Julian. Rather than merely adding a leap year every four years, a leap year is added every year that is divisible by four, except for years that are also divisible by 100 but not divisible by 400. It all stems from the fact that the tropical year, which is the mean duration between the vernal equinoxes, has been measured to be 365.242190 days long instead of 365.25. With the latter number, they could have easily avoided their calendar and leap year gymnastics, Sam mused. Even as those gymnastics are not entirely precise, they will likely serve them quite well for some time to come, before the modern methods of timekeeping fall by the wayside, just as their predecessors before them.

According to the Gregorian leap year formula, the outplayed planetary energy states identified in the Gregorian calendar as years AD 2000 and AD 1600 would have been leap years. Those planetary energy states identified as AD 1700, AD 1800, and AD 1900 would not have been leap years, as they are divisible by 100 but not divisible by 400. All other years between AD 1600 and AD 2000 that were divisible by four would have been leap years.

Using the preceding leap year formula, in the Gregorian calendar 97 years out of every 400 are leap years. Sam scanned the unplayed energy states of AD 2100, AD 2200, AD 2300, and AD 2400. The Gregorian calendar still held, as only AD 2400 out of those four was considered a leap year. But time as understood by humans was undergoing a major transformation by AD 2400. There also was less argumentation about whether it should be called AD 2400 or 2400 CE. Sam was almost surprised to view the underlying causes of that transformation. Despite their scientific prowess in bringing forth the understanding of time, the effects of the timeless longings of their poets and literary geniuses played a major role in acceptance of additional dimensions and transcendence of the scientific method in acquiring knowledge and understanding.

Time: The Literary Perspective

Nowhere in human endeavors is the personal license in describing or referencing time more pronounced than in literature. Sam was reluctant, at first, to scan for the literary meaning of time. After all, the nature of NTP seemed more related to their scientific concept of time. But he knew their science was ultimately a dead-end street and a box. And whereas poetic and literary descriptions of time might not have the respectability of their scientific counterparts among them, Sam was deeply aware that in many instances their poets actually understood the nature of time better than their scientists. The scientists have something to learn from the poets, he mused. He executed a scan. The results were overwhelming. He became absorbed in the poetic feeling of time.

"Even Such Is Time" by Sir Walter Raleigh

Even such is time that takes in trust
Our youth, our joys, our all we have,
And pays us but with age and dust,
Who in the dark and silent grave,
When we have wondered all our ways,
Shuts up the story of our days.
But from this earth, this grave, this dust,
My God shall raise me up, I trust.

Sam noted that Raleigh was a participant in the same planetary energy state in which Pope Gregory the XIII played his role. But Raleigh was much too busy with explorations and being imprisoned in the Tower of London to fully appreciate the calendar change that took place. He seems to have a sense of being an actor, though. And his perception of time as robber of youth and deliverer of death should earn him a role where he can transcend it. He might be a good candidate to advance the NTP transcendence component, Sam mused.

Sonnet 64 by William Shakespeare

When I have seen by Time's fell hand defaced
The rich-proud cost of outworn buried age;
When sometime lofty towers I see down-razed,
And brass eternal slave to mortal rage;
When I have seen the hungry ocean gain
Advantage on the kingdom of the shore,
And the firm soil win the wat'ry main,
Increasing store with loss, and loss with store;
When I have seen such interchange of state,
Or state itself confounded to decay;
Ruin itself hath taught me thus to ruminate—
That Time will come and take my love away.
This thought is as a death, which cannot choose
But weep to have that which it fears to lose.

Sonnet 123 by William Shakespeare

No, Time, thou shalt not boast that I do change!
Thy pyramids built up with newer might
To me are nothing novel, nothing strange;
They are but dressings of a former sight.
Our dates are brief, and therefore we admire
What thou dost foist upon us that is old;
And rather make them born to our desire
Than think that we before have heard them told.
Thy registers and thee I both defy,
No wondering at the present or the past;
For thy records and what we see do lie,
Made more or less by thy continual haste.
This I do vow, and this shall ever be,
I will be true, despite thy scythe and thee.

Sam was not surprised by Shakespeare's grasp of time. In some of his former roles Sam was apprenticed to this masterful actor. NTP was on a distant horizon when Shakespeare was on the earthly stage. Yet, Shakespeare is already talking about the registers of time.

"The New Year" by John Greenleaf Whittier

The wave is breaking on the shore—
The echo fading from the chime—
Again the shadow moveth o'er
The dial-plate of time!

O, seer-seen Angel! Waiting now
With weary feet on sea and shore,
Impatient for the last dread vow
That time shall be no more!

Once more across thy sleepless eye
The semblance of a smile has passed:
The year departing leaves more nigh
Time's fearfullest and last. . . .

Complex transformations took place in the planetary energy states during Whittier's act. Notable players came and left. Sam sadly noted the premature exit of Abraham Lincoln. The NTP horizon was drawing closer still, and Whittier's "echo fading from the chime" was clearly a veiled attempt to advance the concept of truechimers and falsetickers. Here is another one for the "future" NTP team, Sam whispered.

The Mysteries of Time

The greatest of human mysteries are time related. Did Troy exist? Where did it stand? What really happened on that fateful day of November 22, 1963, in Dallas, Texas? There are plenty of other mysteries spawning conspiracy theories and confusion. From the relativity of earthly time the arguments regarding the nature of those "mysterious" planetary energy states will never end. The memory dimension holds the answer. The memory dimension becomes accessible through the transcendence of time. NTP holds the key to transcendence. NTP clocks will have the option of ticking into the "past." They will have the option to interface with viewing and projection systems that allow for an unerring display and replay of any planetary energy state, regardless of its relationship to the human concept of time. "AD 2400" illuminated brightly on Sam's viewing screen.

CHAPTER 2

■ ■ ■

Network Administration and IT Trends Throughout History!

Ere the Big Bang eruption and before time was, NTP already existed as a component of a "future" planetary energy state. The actions of the countless energy transformations that molded NTP into the currently configurable condition have not, in the least, diminished its pre–Big Bang reality. Sam was absorbed in tracing through the seemingly infinite number of energy transformations that were part of NTP's unfoldment since the fiery explosion. What a journey! he exclaimed. The primordial causes that were set in motion at the time of the big burst have not yet fully outplayed themselves. The NTP design is not yet complete, or, better yet, it's not yet fully outpictured! But the recognition on the part of the designers for a strong crypto security and the autoconfiguration capability represents a turning point in NTP's forward march toward its climactic moment of full maturity within the framework of network administration.

Unbreakable NTP security must be in place to prevent the disruption not only of the current global Internet but of the unfolding Interplanetary Internet as well. And the auto-configuration capability—not just for NTP but also for any protocol—has been the dream of network administrators since the earliest beginnings of this ancient profession. Fortunately, time appears to be on the designers' side to reach NTP's fullest potential. There are still numerous energy transformations to be outplayed before the Big Bang transits into the Big Collapse and the fullness of NTP's architecture, configuration options, and troubleshooting techniques compresses once again into a single point of time-transcending existence. There will not be a need for any further enhancements at that point! Not until the next Big Bang, that is!

The Prehistoric Times

The crutch of counting time has allowed the modern-day earthly historians and archeologists to take the continuous panorama of planetary energy transformations and conveniently segment them into historical compartments. The prehistoric times, which represent the period of Earth's history that antedates the development of writing, are one of those compartments.

In the context of the Big Bang scenario, which is estimated to have taken place some 15 billion years ago, and the fact that writing is considered to have emerged from Mesopotamia about 3200 BC (approximately 5,200 years ago), the prehistoric times account for about 99.99996% ((1 – (5,200/15,000,000,000)) * 100%) of the various stages of earthly existence since the big explosion. Conversely, from the perspective of the current earthly dwellers, however long the period of time may appear to be since the invention of writing, it represents only a minute fraction (0.00004%) of the total elapsed time since that memorable moment when the blueprints for all of the networking protocols (including NTP!) suddenly emerged from a single point of compressed energy.

Sam observed that network administration that explicitly incorporates NTP configuration and troubleshooting into its spectrum of activities has been experiencing a considerable acceleration (an increasing rate of change!) since the first four nodes of the ARPAnet (the precursor of the Internet) were connected in AD December 1969 (some 36 years ago as of the time of this writing). He also mused on the parallels in the numerical proportions between the duration of the Internet-era period vs. the "written history" period as contrasted with the "written history" period vs. the prehistoric times.

The Internet-era period represents but a fraction of the segment of time since the invention of writing—approximately 0.7% ((1 – (36/5,200)) * 100%), just as the "written history" period is but a minute fraction of the duration of the prehistoric times. Yet, it is within this fraction of a fraction of time that NTP has experienced the greatest acceleration in the outpicturing of its design, which as a nascent blueprint was already contained within that single point of compressed energy of 15 billion years ago. It's left up to the reader to calculate what percentage of time the Internet-era period represents since the Big Bang.

During the prehistoric times, or even during the 99.3% of time elapsed since the invention of wiring to the beginning of the Internet era, network topologies and administration methods did not entirely resemble the LANs and WANs of today. However, the ongoing planetary energy transformations during those periods were gradually and steadfastly laying a solid groundwork for the current state of networking and the fullness of NTP design.

The prehistoric networks had more to do with the creation of ingenious methods of irrigation (to facilitate greater food production for the expanding populations) than with the use of fiber and satellite links to facilitate high-speed connectivity between the earthly continents for the purpose of e-mail and voice communications. Water, rather than Ethernet frames, flowed through the physical transmission media! Clearly, the user requirements mandated the nature of network implementations even in those times!

Consider a quote from *Past Worlds: Atlas of Archeology*:

> *In Mesopotamia, . . . the annual floods of the Tigris and Euphrates were insufficient, and **costly networks of radial canals** had to be constructed and maintained. . . . The earliest known irrigation canals are in Mesopotamia, dating from around 5000 BC.*

Furthermore, the same publication asserts that during the three millennia from 4000 to 1000 BC, which bridge the prehistoric times to the age of recorded history, "Societies became more *hierarchical*."

Thus, the key concepts of the networking topologies and hierarchy that feature so prominently in NTP design were already in full bloom in the prehistoric times, gathering more momentum during the successive epochs and civilizations. No wonder the kinetic energy that accumulated within those concepts through the ongoing planetary energy transformation has been sufficient to propel the NTP development even further to its current level of cryptographic security and autoconfiguration! And given the gathering momentum of the uninvited and unwelcome practices of hacking and network crashing that are here today and are still to follow into the future, that development is occurring none too soon!

Ancient Greece

The city-states dotting the landscape of ancient Greece reminded Sam of the NTP server farms that were populating some of the more hospitable planets and moons of the solar system in AD 2300. He snapped back from the "future." After all, in order to get there, their activities during the next few centuries must remain congruent with the NTP blueprints dating back to the Big Bang and before. And that's not a small task for the earthlings! All too frequently they lose the vision of the big goals before them! Sam refocused on the planetary states of ancient Greece.

The Networking Aspects of the Trojan War

Various networking topologies, hierarchical principles, turf warfare, and hacking were alive and well not only among the city-state dwellers of ancient Greece but also among their Olympian overseers. Zeus was the undisputed hierarch for the network of Olympian gods who in turn presided over the various areas of human activities, thus setting the pattern for the structure of modern IT departments. And job security was a serious consideration in those days as well!

According to a legend pertaining to events that ultimately led to the Trojan War, Zeus cast his eye at one time upon a beautiful maiden called Thetis, a daughter (one of fifty!) of the sea god Nereus, also known as the Old Man of the Sea. Zeus, however, quickly abandoned his intentions with respect to Thetis when he discovered that, according to prophesies, the male offspring of Thetis should become greater than his father. Clearly, Zeus did not want to lose his position as the supreme hierarch of the Olympian gods. Neither are today's CIOs eager to hire IT personnel who have the potential to replace them.

Thetis was married instead to a hero called Peleus. The wedding of Thetis and Peleus (not unlike the merging of networks with different routing protocols and drastically vary-ing approaches to network administration) was well attended by the gods (IT folks like to party!), including the uninvited Goddess of Discord and Strife, Eris. Sam smiled with concern at the situation. He already knew that IT mergers are challenging to begin with, without an intentional distracter such as Eris spawning intrigue and trying to crash them!

Eris might well qualify as a sponsor and a patroness of today's hackers, spammers, and inside IT saboteurs, he thought. Her beautiful Apple of Discord that she threw upon a table at the wedding banquet carried an inscription, "To the Fairest" (a goddess, that is!).

Note There's no reason for anyone to get upset here on the grounds of sex discrimination in the workplace! This is a wedding in ancient Greece that's being attended by a pantheon of gods and goddesses, not a meeting of a modern-day IT department!

The use of the Apple of Discord by Eris was a ploy masking a spoofing attack against the budding merger between Peleus and Thetis and against the resulting offspring. The implications of Eris's action were traumatic not only at the level of nations and civilizations but they reverberate through the practices of network administration to this day. Her act set in motion causes that led not only to the Trojan War and the subsequent founding, rise, and fall of Rome but also to the endless exploits of today's hackers and crackers who, with their viruses, worms, logic bombs, spyware, and Trojans, insinuate themselves—uninvited—into the best-planned and well-intentioned networks, causing strife in IT departments and numerous headaches for network administrators.

The goddesses present at the wedding fell for Eris's ploy, as each one attempted to claim the Apple of Discord for herself. That's not unlike the initial stage of the convergence of the Spanning Tree Protocol (STP) where every switch claims to be the root, Sam mused. In the end, though, hierarchy prevails! he sighed with relief. When Hera, the wife of Zeus; Athena, the warrior goddess of arts and crafts, learning, wisdom, and the intellect; and Aphrodite, the goddess of love and beauty, also claimed the Apple, all of the lesser goddesses stepped back from it.

But there can be only a single root bridge in any STP configuration, Sam kept reminding himself, as he viewed the trio of powerful goddesses reaching for the Apple! Although, he pondered, instead of STP, they might be setting a pattern here for a distributed hierarchy of stratum 1 NTP servers. Maybe, just maybe, each goddess could be satisfied with a portion of the apple, where they could view themselves as peers with respect to their beauty. Or, perhaps they might also be laying the groundwork for the per-VLAN spanning tree (PVST), where multiple root bridges are possible in a multi-VLAN internetwork! Sam continued to follow the quickly changing energy states at the wedding.

Given the commanding stature and hierarchical position of the three beings now claiming the apple, none of the other attending gods and goddesses wanted to arbitrate between them in order to decide which one, indeed, was the fairest among them. Once again, Sam observed at work here the principle of job security in IT departments! Why rock the boat with the boss over looks?

A naïve prince, Paris, the son of King Priam of Troy, was chosen instead to make the decision as to who would lay the final claim to the apple and thus be considered the fairest. Not only did the goddesses appear to Paris in their resplendent beauty, but each also made a promise to him (a bonus of sorts for those late-at-night or weekend installations and configurations!) to help secure the winning vote. Hera promised him power and riches, Athena glory, and Aphrodite the love of the most beautiful woman in the world at that time. Poor fellow! It was now time for him to do the final configuration of the bridge priority and/or NTP stratum levels. There was not going to be a distributed NTP hierarchy or PVST in this scenario. There was going to be only one winner!

Paris chose Aphrodite and her offering. But there was a serious problem with his choice. Helen, the most beautiful woman of those times, as promised to Paris by Aphrodite, was already married to the king of Sparta, Menelaus. That's not unlike an already overloaded Unix server being chosen to act also as a stratum 1 NTP server as well, Sam murmured, anticipating an imminent crash. But Paris was determined to proceed and was undeterred in claiming his bonus.

When with Aphrodite's assistance Paris visited Sparta as a guest of Menelaus and subsequently repaid his host's generosity by kidnapping Helen and taking her with him to Troy, Menelaus called upon his former rivals for Helen's hand to aid him. They reluctantly complied and soon sailed for Troy. The war was on. The firewalls of Troy ultimately succumbed to the treachery of the Trojan horse constructed by the Greeks. The Achaean hackers prevailed against the audacious Paris attempting to hide his stolen goods inside the private network. Helen eventually returned to Sparta with Menelaus. But that event occurred only after a 10-year bloody battle that fascinates so many to this day and whose authenticity seems to elude the greatest of historians and archeologists. Sam smiled again. He knew that time was on the side of those seeking to know what really took place at Troy and when. But first things first! NTP must manifest its full design before the clocks will be able to tick backward with unerring precision to reveal the past!

Sparta vs. Athens (Determinism vs. Creative Chaos)

The regimented and deterministic Spartan code of 2,500+ years ago that controlled the lives of Sparta's citizens from cradle to grave may well be considered as the ancient precursor to the highly deterministic LAN access method of Token Ring. In Athens, the democratic chaos paved the way for Ethernet instead. Today's networking landscape suggests that, as a function of time, the democratic experiment prevailed over governmental heavy-handedness.

Spartan militarism and determinism already flourished for decades before the Athenian democratic experiment fully began to take hold under the visionary Pericles in 480 BC. IBM was already shipping 4/16Mbps Token Ring controllers in 1989, a full year before the IEEE adopted the 802.3i/10Base-T standard in 1990. The tug-of-war and competition between Sparta and Athens continued for centuries. Fortunately for the modern-day network administrators, the rivalry between Ethernet and Token Ring has been much shorter. When Spartan militarism eventually declined following the battle at Leuctra in 371 BC, there were not too many mourners over Sparta's fate among the other Greek city-state peers. In the Ethernet-dominated LAN networking of today, no one particularly misses Token Ring either, despite its rise to considerable prominence in the financial industry during the decade of the 1990s. But to Sparta's credit, it too had moments of glory. The Spartan performance and sacrifice at Thermopylae in 480 BC, under the leadership of their king Leonidas I, survives as an enduring example of Spartan heroism and bravery.

Surprisingly, though, the Spartan regimentation did little to help the Spartans with accurate timekeeping. And that's despite the opportunities they had to perfect their clocks during Sparta's relatively long period of prosperity and military strength when it was at the helm of the Peloponnesian League from 560 to 380 BC. For example, in 490 BC when all of ancient Greece was threatened by the Persian armies of Darius I—at what's historically considered as the most critical moment for the very survival of the barely flickering flame of Greek freedom—the Spartans were late with their reinforcements to the Athenian and other city-states' armies in the decisive battle of Marathon. The chaotic Athenians managed to defeat the onslaught of tyranny at Marathon, clearing the way for decades of democracy, freedom, and prosperity. The active deployment of 10Gbps switched Ethernet is no doubt a testament to the principles of democracy and chaos in networking, while the Token Ring MAUs have been relegated to the IT junk rooms.

Ancient Rome and the Roman Empire

The history of nations and civilizations is rife with examples of the defeat and destruction of one laying the foundation for the birth of another.

There was at one time a mighty networking giant, Xerox. Remember the Xerox Networking Service (XNS) protocol suite on which another onetime networking giant's (Novell's) IPX/SPX suite was based? Xerox, whose Palo Alto Research Center (PARC) at one time employed Bob Metcalf and David Boggs (the developers of the first experimental Ethernet network in the 1972–1973 time frame!), has been relegated to being a printer and a "toner head" company by the many newcomers to the computing and networking field: Microsoft, Apple, and Novell being chief among them. The newcomers, one and all, immensely benefited from the fruits of the foundational research that had gone on at PARC, notwithstanding their own subsequent unique contributions to the computing and networking arenas.

The Roman poet Virgil in his epic poem, the *Aeneid*, identifies the Romans as having descended from among the defeated Trojans. Unlike Troy, neither PARC was sacked nor Xerox defeated physically (just outsmarted!) by the computing and networking newcomers of the late 1970s and 1980s. It took the Trojans fleeing their burning city—and their subsequent descendents—and more than 400 years of wandering (from 1184 to 753 BC) before they finally settled and founded what became Rome, the city of seven hills that eventually expanded into an empire. It took some of the aggressive newcomers less than a decade to start building their empires on the foundations of Xerox research.

The basis for the seven-layer Open System Interconnection (OSI) reference model can also be traced all the way back to Troy, Sam observed with a sense of wonderment. Romulus well understood network troubleshooting and the development of computing architectures at the time of Rome's founding, he continued to ponder. The city was initially founded on just one hill, the Palatine Hill—the physical layer of the OSI model. The remaining six hills would get their turn later at becoming a part of the Roman networking architecture. The layered approach to network troubleshooting clearly dates back to the earliest days of Rome! Just as current network problems are not solved instantaneously, neither was Rome built nor did it fall in a day!

Sam scanned through the planetary energy states of 1,200+ years during which ancient Rome metamorphosed itself multiple times to eventually become an empire: the entire period from the earliest beginnings of Rome's founding on April 21, 753 BC (a legendary date according to historians still unable to reconstruct the past with accuracy and precision) to the fall of the Western Empire in AD 476. He was struck by the uncanny resemblance between the key epochs in the Roman history (monarchy, republic, and the empire) and the still-unfolding drama of the creation and evolution of the global Internet.

The ARPAnet was born when the first four Interface Message Processors (IMPs) were interconnected between the University of California in Los Angeles (UCLA), the University of California in Santa Barbara (UCSB), the Stanford Research Institute (SRI), and Utah State University (USU), in December 1969. The IMPs were the communication front-ends (router precursors!) to the mainframes and minicomputers resident at the four interconnected institutions. The obscure and now almost legendary ARPAnet lasted as a single network for about 14 years. The most obscure period of the Roman existence, that of its monarchy, lasted a bit longer than the ARPAnet, from 753 to 509 BC, when the Roman Republic was born.

The very restrictive (window of 1) Network Control Protocol (NCP) that was operational on the ARPAnet was dethroned in favor of a more flexible and sliding window–capable TCP/IP beginning January 1, 1983. Later that year, because of security concerns by the Defense Research Agency, the original ARPAnet was split into two networks: Milnet, which carried nonclassified military information, and a scaled-down ARPAnet, which continued to interconnect the various research centers. The two networks were interconnected into a newly emerging and a revolutionary concept at that time, the Internet. The Roman Republic began its existence in 509 BC with two consuls, Lucius Junius Brutus and Lucius Tarquinius Collatius, sharing and checking each other's power instead of having a single, and often tyrannical, restrictive monarch.

The Roman Republic continued its tumultuous existence for almost five centuries until 27 BC, when the Roman Senate afforded the victorious Octavius the title of Augustus, "the consecrated one," elevating him to the status of an emperor and thus bringing the republican era to a close. The transformation of Rome during the republican period affected every aspect of its existence: the form of its government, the laws, and the size of its territory (topology!).

The governance, the protocols, and the topology of the Internet during the period from 1983 through 1995 underwent equally drastic change. The National Science Foundation (NSF) along with the NSFnet dominated the Internet's topological landscape from 1986 to 1995, not unlike the Roman Senate exerting its influence during the republican period in Rome. However, the balance of power on the Internet was well maintained by the emergence and interconnection of the NSFnet with numerous regional networks (MICHnet, SURAnet, BARRnet, PREPnet, MOREnet, and more). Those were the Roman plebeians keeping the patrician-dominated Senate in check!

While no single business entity or institution emerged in 1995 to govern the Internet on the order of the Roman emperors, the geographical breadth and scope of the empire set the pattern for the interconnection of Autonomous Systems (ASs) comprising the modern-day Internet. Among the routing protocols, however, the Border Gateway Protocol (BGP) has clearly risen to imperial preeminence, as it facilitates the cohesion among the thousands of ASs that are in turn comprised of tens of thousands of diverse networks scattered across all of the earthly continents.

And another type of emperor has also emerged on the Internet since 1995 when the NSFnet was decommissioned in favor of the initial four public Network Access Points (NAPs) for peering between the major ISPs: the emperor of commercialization. The ideals of pure science, research, education, and communication that dominated the "republican-era" Internet quickly gave way to the goals of using it as a medium to build vast economic empires.

Since 1995, the Internet has suffered occasional setbacks: panic about running out of registered IP addresses, the growing size of routing tables in the core routers, and routing instabilities. Not unlike the Roman Empire that also suffered occasional setbacks (the great fire of AD 64, civil wars, and many inept emperors), the Internet has continued to recover from all of those challenges. Private addressing in conjunction with Network Address Translation (NAT) and the development of IPv6 are solving the IP address shortage crisis. Routers have become more powerful and capable of handling hundreds of thousands of routes. BGP's route dampening has put the brakes on route flapping and routing instabilities problems.

Sam was optimistic that Internet would not share Rome's ultimate fate—the fall! The hacking vandals will not prevail against the Internet like the Vandals prevailed against the once mighty Rome! That's provided that NTP design, development, and deployment remain secure and on track. The ability of the NTP clocks to run backward in order to review the "past" with precision should be a choice for network administrators rather than a condition that's forced upon them involuntarily. That functionality simply cannot be allowed to be hijacked by the vandal hackers attempting to preempt the ultimate outpicturing of Internet's blueprint. The rebels against the future cannot prevail!

The Middle (Dark) Ages

The Middle Ages are associated with the time period from the fall of the Western Roman Empire (AD 476) through the 15th century AD. The Dark Ages represent approximately the first five centuries of that period. Another 1,000+ years chock-full of events that were to shape the 21st century network administration and IT trends, Sam uttered as the panorama of the Middle Ages energy states unfolded before him. His continued observations led him to conclude that while certain key concepts and network administration techniques have their roots in the Middle Ages, many of the energy states from those times were a significant weight and a drag rather than a propellant for the current unfoldment of innovative networking techniques. He flashed back for a moment to his native orb, where the application of the Universal Solvent (US) to the "past" energy states was a common practice.

The action of the US absolved the "past" states from their out-of-the-blueprint conditions and allowed the "future" states to be more readily outpictured without being affected by the "past." Sam grappled with how the concept of the US could be released to the all-knowing earthlings without an offense to their well-developed reasoning powers. After all, the US was a form of energy that their scientific instruments could not yet register. Or, perhaps, the human reasoning powers are not so developed after all! he continued to muse. The last 3,000+ years since the sacking of Troy are nothing but a continuum of rise and fall of nations and civilizations: Troy, city-states of ancient Greece, the Roman Empire, the ever-changing border topologies of the European nations, and more. What a bunch of yo-yos, he exclaimed! The US could certainly help them with a more steadfast approach to maintaining a continuity of civilization instead of the ups and downs of birth, rise, and fall!

He refocused on the Middle Ages panorama. The fall of the Western Roman Empire in AD 476 was a formality. The decline of the empire that led to the deposing of the last boy emperor, Romulus Augustus (how appropriate that the last emperor should be named after the Rome's founder and the first powerful emperor!), was a process that went on for several centuries before that ceremonial event took place. The fall, however, gave rise to segmentation throughout the empire's topology (a key concept in managing network performance) and through it the eventual emergence of the European nation states. The barbarians who flooded and eventually brought down the Roman Empire set the pattern for the Ethernet broadcast storms that, if unchecked by properly configured STP, can easily "melt down" modern networks. Medieval Europe's network of fortified castles—with their bastions and drawbridges—defines today's firewall technology. The stench of the countless dead from plagues and endless battles of the Middle Age period is quite comparable to the atmosphere that surrounds the many mergers, takeovers, bankruptcies, and dissolutions of the seemingly endless dot-coms.

But Sam was suddenly astounded at what he saw as he drew to conclusion his Middle Ages scans. A few among the Middle Age players were already aware of the US and were applying it quite successfully to some of the "past" energy states. They knew what the "future" held if unencumbered by the past! Those were the Middle Age visionaries energizing the blueprints of the Renaissance, the period of the Industrial Revolution, and the modern times. He was glad to observe a similar vision and US-awareness among the NTP designers and developers of today.

The Industrial Revolution

At best, the "Industrial Revolution" (IR) is a very poor label to describe the varying and not precisely definable (within a second, a day, or even a year!) periods of time in various parts of the world during which a remarkable and a very far-reaching social transformation was taking place. Attempting to define the "Industrial Revolution" in a sentence or two makes almost as much sense as trying to describe the varied aspects of modern-day network administration to a pre–Internet era CEO, Sam quipped.

But, however difficult it might be to define briefly the "Industrial Revolution" or to confine its duration to exact dates (in Britain, specifically, it is being approximated as lasting from about 1750 to about 1850), the activities that took place during its tenure made an indelible impression on modern-day networking. The forces that were unleashed during the periods of the IR ushered major changes in the population distribution (accelerated growth of cities), the means of making money (mostly from manufacturing and commerce rather than agriculture), the movement of goods within and between countries (via railroads and steam ships), and the new techniques of generating and harnessing power (via steam and internal combustion engines).

Aggregation and core routers—switching millions of packets per second and linked by high-speed backbones—are the major population centers of the industrial era exchanging goods via railways. Web hosting, e-commerce, managed data services, and voice over IP (VoIP) are just a smattering of new income streams. And how about those new means of generating and harnessing power? The raw materials for the new power sources were there all along, even during the Middle Ages and before. Sam paused for a moment. NTP has been around now for two decades. The question is, how soon will they be able to recognize it as the key to time transcendence?

The Modern Times

Tens of thousands of websites and numerous documents attribute to Thomas Watson Sr., the onetime chairman of IBM, the famous quote he supposedly made in 1943: "I think there is a world market for maybe five computers." None of those sites offer an explanation of the context in which the alleged remark was made. According to Wikipedia, no evidence exists that Thomas Watson Sr. ever uttered those words. The World History Series publication for young readers by James A. Corrick, *The Industrial Revolution*, attributes a similar comment to Watson Sr. but about seven years later, in 1950, when he was supposedly considering the extremely high cost and maintenance overhead associated with the operation of the monstrosity known as the Electronic Numerical Integrator and Computer (ENIAC).

ENIAC is considered to be the first fully all-electronic computer that was under construction for several years before being formally placed in operation at the Moore School of Electrical Engineering at the University of Pennsylvania in February 1946. ENIAC weighed approximately 30 tons, contained more than 17,000 vacuum tubes, consumed more than 200 kilowatts of power, and had far less capabilities than a modern low-end PC. The demands of the ancient human activity, war (World War II, in this case), drove the development of ENIAC. The initial purpose of ENIAC was to calculate ballistic firing tables. IBM was not in the business of building electronic computers either in 1943, when the initial agreement for the construction of ENIAC was signed between the United States of America and the University of Pennsylvania trustees, or in 1950.

Sam pondered the susceptibility of earthlings to good stories, whether or not they reflect the reality of the planetary energy states they are supposed to describe. A story that's built around someone of stature supposedly making a prediction that does not reflect a future planetary condition is a good story. The tens of thousands of modern-day websites regarding Watson Sr.'s alleged remark are living proof of a good story. But these are supposed to be the modern times where accuracy and precision in timekeeping, communications, and reporting are at their peak! he remarked wryly. As long as the inability to read the past with accuracy and precision remains, the modern-day myths will continue! The NTP designers are on a timeline if the network administrators of subsequent centuries want to know the truth regarding Watson Sr.'s remark!

More than a half a century after the alleged remark by Watson Sr. was made, the famed founder of Digital Equipment Corporation (DEC), Ken Olson, asserted in 1977, "There is no reason anyone would want a computer in their home." Both statements (whether actually made or not!) are drastically wrong as a function of time. But they make a good story. And in no way does any alleged lack of insight into the future by Watson Sr. and Olson detract from their tremendous contributions to the field of computing and networking. They presided at the helm of two of the most renowned and innovative computer companies of modern times. IBM survived; DEC was dismembered and assimilated by others. But on their shoulders—and those of countless others—the global revolution in networking continues apace.

Since the days of the famous quote (or misquote!) by Watson Sr., hundreds of millions of business and home computers now populate the planet, the vast majority of them linked to the Internet. Monarchical network administration of the late 1970s and the 1980s has been dethroned, commercialized, and fully democratized. Internet, routers, firewalls, and IP addressing and subnetting have become household words. The number of RFCs exceeds 4,000. The seeds of networking that have been planted since the ancient times are now in full bloom. But the NTP visionaries know that they still have a major challenge before them. Is the networking world ready to find out for fact what Watson Sr. really said and when?

PART 2

NTP: The Story Behind the Accuracy and Synchronization of Network Time

CHAPTER 3

■■■

NTP Operational, Historical, and Futuristic Overview

Not unlike the physical theories with their supporting time-dependent equations, communications between networking devices rely on time as well. Throughout this and subsequent chapters, the classical physics view of time is assumed. The reader is referred to Chapter 1 for additional perspectives on the concept of time, which permeates the operations of numerous networking protocols, not just NTP.

Various timers and time interval parameters (update, invalid, holddown, flush, hello, dead, wait, retransmit, keepalive, and more) exist within routing and other protocols such as ICMP, RIP, IRGP, OSPF, and BGP. Network administrators need to be familiar with the actions of these time-related parameters and configure them judiciously. Those parameters are—almost without exception—absolutely integral to the proper functioning of the protocols. Inexperienced tinkering with protocol timers can lead to disasters on the order of bringing down entire networks.

As a general rule, and given the obsession with performance in computing environments, the faster-performing protocols are preferred over their slower counterparts. This is unless, of course, the faster protocols are not supported because of networking device positioning for a specific market segment or the inability of a specific line of networking hardware to support a high-performance protocol's operational requirements. Network administrators may also sideline the faster protocols in favor of their slower counterparts when they prove to be more difficult to configure and maintain than their slower counterparts. This is especially true in deployments where the higher protocol performance results in minimal if any benefit to the overall network operations.

However, in any respectable mission-critical internetworking scenario, a routing protocol with fast convergence is deemed preferable over its slower sibling, as it allows a multipath network to become operational faster after a failure of one or more network links. The same high-performance networking requirements that bring about the development and deployment of faster routing protocols also apply to NTP with regard to maintaining increasingly accurate time synchronization on ever more complex multi-OS networks. There are now multiple operational versions of NTP, as the protocol has grown in sophistication and capabilities over the last two decades. At the same time, the emergence of the Simple Network Time Protocol (SNTP) clearly indicates that the high performance and precision of the latest NTP is not necessary or even desirable in all networking environments.

■**Note** The simple truth regarding NTP is that since its inception the protocol has evolved and developed a granularity of performance and configuration to accommodate a wide range of networking environments, from the simplest to the most complex.

In addition to the networking protocols being time dependent, real-time communications (as the name itself implies!) are time dependent as well. They rely on time delays in certain ranges (from tens to a few hundreds of milliseconds) in order to be acceptable to the participants. Those delays are short compared to the timers and intervals that facilitate communication among networking devices and that are often measured in seconds or minutes. Regardless of the level of supported or required time granularity during the communication process between humans and/or computing devices, one thing is clear: the means of time measurement must be agreed upon between them. The time mechanism of choice for computer networking and NTP is now the Coordinated Universal Time (UTC). The unique characteristics of UTC are that it is a 24-hour clock system and that any given moment UTC is the same no matter where you are located on the planet. The local clocks in different time zones may differ by many hours; however, if networking devices that are located in those time zones are synchronized to UTC, then UTC on those devices will be the same.

NTP: What, Why, and How?

Attempts at network timekeeping precede NTP. In what may seem like an eternity ago in the networking world, in May 1983, J. Postel and H. Harrenstein published a two-page RFC entitled the "Time Protocol." RFC 868 specified a very simple time protocol that could operate as a service on top of either UDP or TCP. The time protocol uses port 37 to listen to requests and returns a 32-bit value of time, which is represented in seconds since 00:00, midnight, on January 1, 1900, Greenwich Mean Time (GMT). Given the capacity of a 32-bit number, this simple time protocol will likely require some adjustments by the year 2036.

■**Note** Consider that out of the 137 years between 1900 and 2036 inclusive, 34 are leap years (see Chapter 1 for a closer discussion of leap years in the Gregorian calendar). This means there are 137 * 365 + 34, or 50,039, days in that time interval. Given that there are 86,400 seconds in a day, the interval yields 4,323,369,600 seconds, which is more than the highest value of 4,294,967,295 for a decimal number that can be represented via a 32-bit binary number. Whereas the year 2036 may seem far away, it's a matter of time before it's here and the implication of a 32-bit number representing timestamps in seconds since January 1, 1900, will have to be considered by applications programmers and network administrators of that and future years.

In September 1985, two years after RFC 868 was published, Dave Mills published the first in a series of RFCs that specify the Network Time Protocol, RFC 958. Efforts at enhancing NTP and making it applicable and relevant in the rapidly changing networking environment have continued ever since.

What Is NTP?

NTP is one of the application services protocols within the TCP/IP suite. As such, NTP finds itself among the company of the TCP/IP workhorses that include Telnet, FTP, SNMP, SMTP, and more. NTP has been assigned the well-known port number 123, and NTP implementations rely on UDP for transport services. Despite NTP's membership in the dominant TCP/IP suite, the protocol can be adapted to and incorporated into other protocol stacks. The fundamental purpose of NTP is extremely simple: time synchronization among participating network devices with reference to a reliable clock source. Generically, from the network administration perspective, a reliable NTP clock source could be either absolute or relative.

An *absolute* clock source represents the planetary time, as accurately as it is humanly possible to measure it. In practice, the absolute clock source represents UTC, typically originating from a Global Positioning System (GPS) satellite, a radio station operated by the U.S. National Institute of Standards and Technology (NIST), or radio stations in other countries sourcing UTC. The three radio stations that are operated by NIST have been assigned call letters WWV, WWVB, and WWVH. WWV and WWVB are located near Fort Collins, Colorado, while WWVH is located on the island of Kauai, Hawaii. UTC is based on the atomic timescale, where the definition of a second is a function of the properties of the cesium-133 atom (see the section "Definition of an Atomic Second" in Chapter 1). Since the atomic timescale differs slightly from the astronomical timescale that is based on Earth's rotation, a leap second is periodically inserted into UTC (about four seconds in the course of every five years!) in order to keep UTC synchronized with the astronomical (also referred to as the *navigational*) timescale.

■**Note** In the context of NTP, the network administrator's absolute clock source is referred to as the *primary reference source*. An NTP server that sources its time via GPS or from a NIST radio station incorporates a primary reference source and is referred to as a *primary timeserver*, or a *stratum 1 server*. In turn, a primary reference source is often referred to as just a *reference clock*. Not all NTP devices are capable of supporting a primary reference source, or a reference clock, even as all NTP devices will have a local clock. The radio stations and GPS satellites that source UTC are referred to as *external reference sources*.

A *relative* clock source represents a time on a device with which all of the other networking devices must synchronize but that time is not derived from or synchronized with a UTC source. It could simply be the time on a networking device that has been arbitrarily set by a network administrator to approximate the time of an electric clock that's located on a wall within a building where the network is deployed. Ironically, a device could be configured as a stratum 1 without deriving its time from UTC. This practice is generally not recommended, but it is also not discouraged as long as the network administrator is aware of its implications. See Chapter 5 for more details on various approaches to NTP configuration.

From an installation and configuration perspective, NTP is a client/server application. The NTP algorithms may already be incorporated into a computing device's (router, switch, server, workstation) operating system, or they may be within an add-on program or module. If NTP is already incorporated into the OS, then it's a matter of determining whether the OS supports both the server and the client functions and proceeding accordingly with configuration. If additional software is required to install NTP, always consider the network administration issue of software compatibility and interoperability and the mechanics of installing and maintaining a client/server application on a network. For example, client software may be required on user workstations to synchronize them with a dedicated stratum 1 timeserver (see the section "Step 1: Choosing Your NTP Time Source" in Chapter 5 for a discussion of dedicated timeservers). On the other hand, no additional software is required on routers and switches to configure them either as NTP clients or as higher stratum servers.

The impact of having or not having the clock synchronization among networking devices becomes a function of the network use and size. In order to determine the most appropriate NTP deployment scenario, the implications of inaccurate timekeeping and/or lack of time synchronization should be arrived at by network administrators through risk analysis, which in turn is part of the NTP design process that should always be conducted prior to NTP deployment!

Why the Need for NTP?

NTP configuration is not required for a networking device to function. Every router or switch has its own local clock, and network administrators are free to set the device clocks to the time that appears on their watches at the time of configuration.

A household with multiple clocks each showing a different time may function quite well until an event occurs (usually catastrophic) that requires an exact identification in time. If an act of vandalism, or worse, is linked by the victim to an inaccurate time of day or night (an earlier or a later time than the actual time at the location of the act), and the suspect can produce an alibi of being elsewhere at the reported time, then, with no other hard evidence linking the suspect to the crime, the case may collapse. The same concept applies to networking and time synchronization on the network. Every router, switch, server, or workstation can have its own time until one of the following takes place:

- An event occurs that requires the reconstruction of other past events with respect to time.

- An event does not take place because it was dependent on other events that should have been executed in a specific time sequence but were not because of lack of time synchronization or the wrong time.

A multitude of consequences can potentially stem from the preceding scenarios, thus adding credence to the saying "Timing is everything," even in networking!

Given the permeation of computer networks and networking solutions in most business operations in the modern world, the value of accurate and synchronized time among networking devices is gradually assuming increasing importance. Consider, for example, the effects of lack of time synchronization in executing stock market trades.

A request comes in from a client to execute a trade within a specified period of time. If different devices are involved in the process of receiving the request and executing the trade, lack of time synchronization between them could result in the perception based on unreliable timestamps that the trade was not executed in the time frame specified by the request. Assuming the lack of satisfaction with the trade on the part of the client, along with the perception that instructions were not followed as requested, potential financial and legal implications are associated with the preceding scenario. While the discussion of these implications is outside the scope of this book, it may be comforting for traders to know that brokerage firms are subject to regulatory requirements regarding the time synchronization on their networks.

The inability to reconstruct past network events (a form of computer forensics) with respect to a reliable time source may result, for example, in the inability to identify the sequence of events during a security breach. That, in turn, may result in the inability to put effective countermeasures in place. However, put the security breach scenario in perspective. A network administrator who considers his or her network as being fully protected against potential attacks from the inside or the outside may not be overly concerned about the lack of time synchronization on his or her network with respect to network security.

But assume for a moment that there are time-dependent operational activities that need to take place on that network. Given the absence of any mechanism to implement time synchronization on this "secure" network, all of the networking devices and servers are operating based on the time configured into them by the network administrator. And given the growing number of devices and the fact that the network administrator happens to be on overload, it's natural to expect that because of human error in time setting as well as the "drifting" of the clocks on the individual devices, time synchronization on that network will suffer as a function of time.

The operational activities on the network could include data backups, data archiving, printing of reports, or virus scanning, for example. Without getting too much into the issues of network management, consider a scenario where a nightly data backup does not occur because of a wrong time on the network. A system crash follows in the morning. In a business that's heavily transaction oriented, all of the transaction data from the previous day is lost. The impact of the loss can be extremely costly in terms of the amount of extra time that's required to reenter the lost data (if it's even possible), the resulting delays in processing customer orders, and the potential customer relations problems because of an inability to handle new requests properly. With time synchronization, the backup server would not have missed the timed backups, even if initially it ended up with an incorrect time configured by a tired network administrator.

On the other hand, time synchronization may be completely irrelevant for a home office network that consists of a couple of PCs and an Internet access router where backups are executed manually to a memory stick, a CD-RW, or even a floppy disk. However, should a legal dispute erupt between the home business and its client, and the exact timing of communications or commercial exchanges between them over the Internet is deemed critical to resolving the dispute, the home office business might suffer a legal loss as a result of not having its PC clocks synchronized to an accurate and reliable time source.

The case for NTP deployment becomes very compelling when business requirements that demand accurate and synchronized timekeeping have been clearly identified. The reader can only imagine the criticality of the time synchronization and accurate time-keeping requirement on networks in manufacturing environments that involve chemicals, food, pharmaceutical products, or even consumer-category electronic equipment. Starting an industrial process at a wrong time, or performing the process for a wrong amount of time, can result in a final product that's outside the acceptable tolerances. In the case of human consumables that are subjected to processes in an incorrect sequence or for a wrong duration of time, there is the potential for dire health consequences for the consumers and legal consequences for the manufacturers.

Thus, on a complex network with hundreds of devices that are interdependent with respect to time, time synchronization and accurate timekeeping become critical components of the overall network operations and management. When network operation is subject to the undesirable effects of cascading events that are due either to an overt initial occurrence (a security breach, for example) or to the omission of an event that's supposed to initiate a sequence of desirable actions, being able to reconstruct events correctly with respect to time gives an administrator a better chance at implementing effective corrective actions.

How Does NTP Operate?

The effect of NTP operations on a network is simple and straightforward: accurate time synchronization among the configured devices. The NTP algorithms, however, are quite complex in order to support the seemingly simple end result. Maintaining time synchronization on the network sounds simple in principle. But consider the nature of networking:

- An internetwork may be composed of numerous routers, switches, and servers from different vendors running different versions of operating systems, even from the same vendor. Thus, NTP implementations must be interoperable across a wide spectrum of vendors, operating systems, and types of computing devices.

- Multiple WAN links of varying capacities may be introducing varying levels of delays into the network traffic, including the NTP messages. Thus, the NTP algorithm must take into account the very nature of the network on which it operates, including the potential for use of asymmetric paths between the communicating devices.

- One of the NTP time sources may have been compromised and is communicating the wrong time. If network security cannot be assured through other means, NTP itself must be able to detect the falseticker and also ensure secure time synchronization exchanges in a scalable manner.

All of the preceding issues—and more—must out of necessity be considered when designing and enhancing NTP, even as separate configuration and operational issues become relevant during NTP deployment.

NTP Deployment Concepts

Every device on the network can potentially participate in NTP exchanges. The manner in which a device participates in NTP will determine its mode of operation. The mode field inside of the NTP message (see the subsequent "NTP Messages" section) identifies how a device (generically, an NTP host) participates in NTP synchronizations.

NTP and Routing

To facilitate NTP operational scalability and redundancy, network administrators should consider deploying NTP in a manner that logically resembles the network routing model. For example, a single NTP server may be sufficient for a one-subnet network just as a single access router often services single subnets. But, as the number of subnets in an internetwork multiplies, configuring an NTP server on just one subnet and expecting all of the clients from all of the remaining subnets to synchronize with it offers no redundancy and becomes less and less scalable.

In complex internetworks, the routing configuration typically follows the logical topology of a distributed hierarchy. Core routers peer with one another and exchange routing updates with a layer of lower-tier routers. As a function of size and throughput requirements, a network may be deployed with multiple layers of lower-tier routers. In that scenario, the NTP logical topology could approximate the logical routing topology with the NTP physical topology approximating the physical distribution of routers. It might be entirely appropriate to configure some of the routers as NTP servers, keeping in mind their anticipated traffic load.

The Hierarchical Nature of NTP

NTP, by its very nature, is a hierarchical protocol, with the NTP servers being identified by a stratum number. The higher the stratum number assigned to an NTP server, the further the server is removed from the primary reference source (a clock that's synchronized with UTC via GPS, CDMA, or a NIST radio station), which conversely means that the lower the stratum number, the closer the server to a primary reference source. Note that the stratum number has nothing to do with physical proximity between the servers or the physical location of the higher stratum servers with respect to the primary reference source. Rather, the stratum number facilitates a logical configuration of the servers that in turn defines and identifies the hierarchical lines of communication between them during the ongoing time synchronization process. However, a stratum 1 server that synchronizes its time with UTC has to be within the physical reach of the UTC transmission mechanism.

The NTP servers with the higher stratum numbers synchronize their time with the lower stratum number servers, while a stratum 1 server synchronizes its time with UTC. Stratum 1 servers can be either public or private. More than a hundred public NTP stratum 1 servers are available on the Internet. For more information about those servers, view the URL http://www.eecis.udel.edu/~mills/ntp/clock1b.html. Also, multiple vendors offer stratum 1 servers for installation on private networks. The GPS stratum 1 servers are quite common for private use, given the extensive worldwide coverage offered by GPS.

A stratum 1 server that is interfaced into the core of a complex network—with the appropriate provisions for redundancy as deemed necessary by the network administrator—could be accompanied by one or more layers of higher stratum servers toward the edges of the network. That logical layout would approximate the routing hierarchy and offer a degree of resiliency without placing undue load on the network bandwidth in the proximity of the stratum 1 server. Figure 3-1 illustrates the concept of NTP hierarchy.

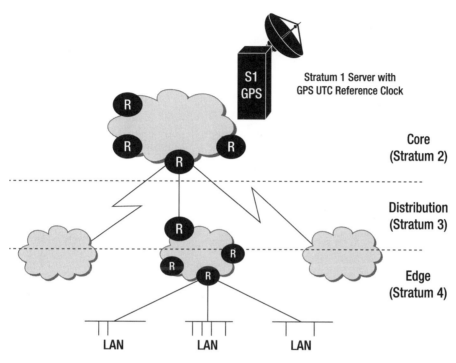

Figure 3-1. *Hierarchical nature of NTP*

In Figure 3-1, the stratum 1 server with a primary reference source is interfaced into the core of the network. Core routers are configured as stratum 2 servers, distribution routers as stratum 3 servers, and edge routers as stratum 4 servers. End-user devices on the LANs are all NTP clients. This topology distributes the NTP synchronization traffic throughout the network layers instead of concentrating all of the traffic in the direction of the stratum 1 server.

A key NTP deployment consideration is to determine whether all of the network devices are going to participate in the NTP exchanges. If only the internetworking devices (routers and switches) are required to maintain synchronization and the network administrator is not concerned about the end-user devices (workstations) remaining synchronized, the NTP deployment model could be further simplified. Logically, the deployment model could end up being a collapsed topology where all of the networking devices are synchronizing with a stratum 1 server. In Figure 3-1, all of the core, distribution, and edge routers could be configured as clients of the stratum 1 server.

NTP Messages

The nature of a protocol and its operations can often be best understood by reviewing the structure of its messages. NTP relies on the use of two types of messages: data and control. Since NTP is an application services protocol, the NTP messages are encapsulated within the IP packet immediately following the UDP header. NTP messages carry mostly data that's used by the time synchronization algorithms. Optionally, the NTP message contains security-related fields.

NTP Data Messages

The NTP version 3 data message includes the following fields:

Leap indictor (2-bit indicator): This is not a leap year indicator but rather a leap second indicator. UTC relies on the atomic clock that defines a second as being equal in duration to 9,192,631,770 oscillations, or cycles, that take place in the ground state of the cesium-133 atom. UTC is thus an atomic timescale. However, there is also an astronomical timescale that depends on the rate of Earth's rotation about its axis. From the perspective of our everyday lives, Earth's rotation seems to be slowing down by an incredibly small amount per year, less than one atomic second. However, this implies that the definition of a second according to an astronomical timescale (1/86,400 of a mean solar day) is going to get slightly longer as a function of time (a long time!). Over the long period of time, there could creep in a discrepancy (in seconds) between the atomic-based UTC and the astronomical timescales. To prevent this from happening, international organizations that deal with weights of measures have agreed that this discrepancy should never be more than a second. Whenever the discrepancy approaches a second, a second is inserted into the UTC timescale. That action takes place on average about four times in the course of five years. The leap second indicator is intended to provide a warning that a leap second will be inserted (or deleted, which has not happened yet!) during the last minute of the day when the indicator is set to binary 01 (for addition) or binary 10 (for deletion).

Version number (3-bit integer): This field represents the NTP version number. As of the time of writing, NTP version 4 implementations are commercially available (or at least vendors claim so!). However, this does not mean that NTP version 4 has been recognized as an Internet standard. A very stringent process applies to the standardization of Internet protocols. This process involves a close cooperation between the Internet Engineering Task Force (IETF) working groups that are responsible for the development of protocol specifications and the Internet Engineering Steering Group (IESG) that is responsible for the technical management of IETF activities and the Internet standards process. Currently, NTP version 2 has been approved as a "standard," NTP version 3 is in a "draft standard" stage, and NTP version 4 has not yet been assigned an RFC number. Commercial protocol implementations normally precede protocol standardization, as the standardization process relies on learning about the peculiarities and characteristics of a protocol through experience. For more information on the protocol standardization process and the current standards, the reader is referred to RFCs 1602 and 1800.

Mode (3-bit integer): This number represents either the type of association that exists between devices exchanging NTP messages and/or a willingness on a part of the NTP host to form an association. Five types of modes have been defined for NTP version 3: symmetric active, symmetric passive, client, server, and broadcast. These mode types correspond to the values of 1 through 5, respectively. The mode values of 6 and 7 are used by NTP control messages. Even though the NTP control messages have a different header structure than the NTP data messages, they share the mode field, and the position of the mode field in the control message headers is the same as in the data messages. A control message is thus identified by the value of 6 or 7 in the last three bits of the first octet of any NTP message, i.e., the mode field. Various parameters that are used with the Unix `restrict` command (in Chapter 5, the section "Typical Unix/Linux Client Configuration" pertains to the actions of the NTP control messages). The mode value of 6 is normally used by the `ntpq` utility, while the mode value of 7 is used by the `ntpdc` utility. The `ntpdc` utility is considered to be more advanced than `ntpq`. Historically speaking, RFC 1305 (published in 1992) reserves the mode value of 7 for private use, which implies that there is not necessarily going to be any kind of standardization for the actions of control messages with the mode value of 7. It's up to the individual vendors or collective groups working on the next versions of NTP to decide how to use the feature of mode value of 7. See Chapter 4 for a more detailed discussion about NTP associations and the operation modes 1 through 5.

Stratum (8-bit integer): The device stratum number. This number indicates how far removed—logically, through configuration in terms of intervening servers—an NTP device is from a UTC clock source. The higher the stratum number, the further the device is removed.

Poll interval (8-bit signed integer): The value represented by this field is the maximum interval in seconds between messages sent by an NTP peer. However, the value of the field is not the number that appears in the field. The value of the field is 2 raised to the power of the number that appears in the field. A 2 in the field yields a value of 4, 3 yields 8, 4 yields 16, etc.

Precision (8-bit signed integer): The value represented by this field indicates the precision of the local clock in seconds or, in practice, a fraction of a second. The represented value is the next largest power of 2 of the actual clock precision value. Similarly, as in the poll interval, the value of the field is a function of the number that appears in the field. The value of the field is equal to 2 raised to the power of the number that appears in the field. Given the fractional nature of the field value, the numbers in the field are negative. Since a clock's precision is related to its frequency, the higher the frequency, the higher the precision and the smaller the value of the field. A precision of 20 ms would be represented by the value of 31.25 ms, which is derived from 2^{-5}, or 1/32. A precision of 1 ms would be represented by the value of 1.95 ms, which is derived from 2^{-9}, or 1/512. Attempting to assign a value of 0.97 ms (2^{-10}, or 1/1024) to a clock with a precision of 1 ms would violate the rule that the value must be the next largest, not the next nearest power of 2.

Root delay (32-bit signed fixed-point number): The value of this field represents in seconds and fractions thereof the total round-trip delay to the primary reference source. With 1 bit allocated to represent the sign, 15 bits allocated to the representation of seconds, and the remaining 16 bits to the fraction of a second, the maximum value that could be represented by this field is between 9 and 10 hours (32,767 seconds). Root delay can assume either a positive value or a negative value as a function of the clock precision and skew. See Chapter 4's "Additional NTP Terms and Definitions" section for definitions of *clock precision* and *skew*.

Root dispersion (32-bit signed fixed-point number): The value of this field represents in seconds and fractions thereof the maximum error relative to the primary reference source. The format of the field is the same as that of root delay with 1 bit representing the sign, 15 bits representing seconds, and the remaining 16 bits representing a fraction of a second. However, this field can assume only positive values.

Reference clock identifier (32-bit code): This field represents the time reference source. For stratum 1 servers, this field takes on the form of a left-justified American Standard Code for Information Interchange (ASCII) string. For stratum 2 servers, this field assumes the value of an IP address of the server. Some of the suggested ASCII strings for stratum 1 servers include WWVH, WWVB, WWV, and GPS. These should be familiar to the reader from the earlier discussion in this chapter on UTC reference sources.

Reference timestamp (64-bit unsigned fixed-point integer): This is the local time in seconds (and fractions thereof!) at which the device clock was last reset or corrected as a result of NTP synchronization operations. The value of this field is zero if the device clock has never been synchronized. Thirty-two bits of this field represent the number of seconds while the remaining 32 bits represent a fraction of a second. With 32 bits representing seconds, it's possible to identify periods of time that span almost 137 years, depending on when that period of time begins (see the calculation for the number of seconds from 1900 through 2036 in the "NTP: What, Why, and How?" section of this chapter). With 32 bits representing a fraction of a second, it's possible to represent accuracy to within hundreds of picoseconds (1 picosecond = 10^{-12} second).

Originate timestamp (64-bit unsigned fixed-point integer): This is the local time at which the client sent a request message to the server, in the same format as the reference timestamp.

Receive timestamp (64-bit unsigned fixed-point integer): This is the local time at which the server received a request message from the client, in the same format as the reference timestamp.

Transmit timestamp (64-bit unsigned fixed-point integer): This is the local time at which the server responded to the request message from the client, in the same format as the reference timestamp.

Authenticator (96 bits): This is an optional field for implementing NTP authentication.

Figure 3-2 illustrates the structure of the NTP message. The numbers at the top of the figure represent bit positions within the message, which is graphically being represented in 32-bit segments, while the numbers in parentheses that follow field descriptions represent the length of the fields in bits.

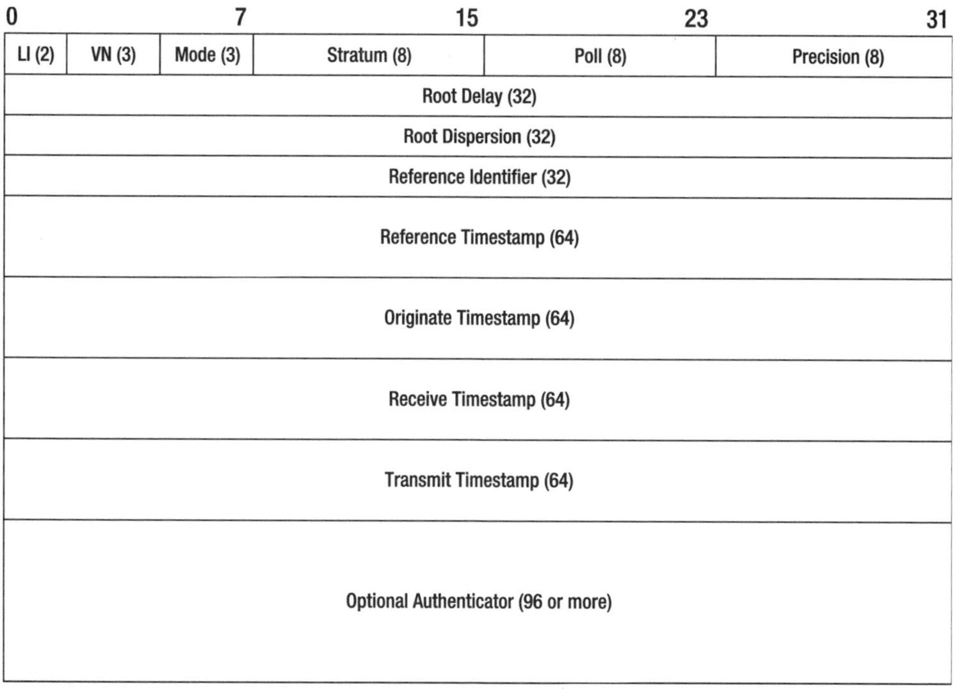

0		7		15		23		31
LI (2)	VN (3)	Mode (3)	Stratum (8)		Poll (8)		Precision (8)	
Root Delay (32)							
Root Dispersion (32)							
Reference Identifier (32)							
Reference Timestamp (64)							
Originate Timestamp (64)							
Receive Timestamp (64)							
Transmit Timestamp (64)							
Optional Authenticator (96 or more)							

Figure 3-2. *Structure of the NTP data message*

The values of the four timestamps in the data message serve as input to the NTP algorithms that allow a client to determine the difference between its own internal time and the primary source reference time and, consequently, adjust its time accordingly. The structure of the NTP message has been evolving through the progression of NTP versions, but the four timestamps have been part of the NTP message since the initial NTP proposal. They represent the core data that facilitate the very purpose of the protocol: accurate timekeeping and synchronization.

NTP Control Messages

The NTP control messages facilitate the execution of control and monitoring functions that might not be available in NTP deployment through the Simple Network Management Protocol (SNMP). Those functions might include, but not be limited to, setting the values of leap-indicator bits, adjusting system parameters, and monitoring NTP operations. The control message structure is quite different from that of the data message, but the first two fields (version number and mode) overlap between the control and data messages. A control message is identified to the NTP software via the value of 6 or 7 in the mode field. The NTP control message contains a 468-octet field that represents the data either in the form of a command to the control message receiver or as a response to a command from a sender. The operation code in the control message that identifies the command function is a 5-bit integer with the potential of 32 values. Only 8 of the 32 values are currently in use with the remaining 24 reserved, clearly indicating the potential for further enhancements of the control message functionality.

Table 3-1 describes the values and the meanings of the operation code, as they are potentially of greatest interest to the network administrators and relate directly to the access control configuration parameters that are used with the `restrict` command in Unix/Linux NTP configurations. The reader is referred directly to RFC 1305 for the entire and exact composition of the NTP control message.

Table 3-1. Operation Code Values in NTP Control Messages

Op Code Value	Operation Code Description
0	Reserved
1	Read status command/response
2	Read variable command/response
3	Write variable command/response
4	Read clock variable command/response
5	Write clock variable command/response
6	Set trap address/port command response
7	Trap response
8–31	Reserved

NTP Versions 1,2, 3, and 4

The presence of multiple NTP versions reflects its ongoing evolution in response to the growing need for accurate and secure network timekeeping and time synchronization between participating devices. For a sense of perspective, consider that the initial NTP proposal that solicited comments and discussion about the fledging protocol (RFC 958) was about 14 pages long, while the NTP version 3 specification has ballooned to about 120 pages. That's close to an order of magnitude increase in the number of pages describing NTP. As no protocol operates on its own in some networking vacuum—but rather in conjunction with others—consider also the nature of a protocol and the underlying work behind it by the number of references to other work and protocols in the specification documents. The initial NTP proposal has 13 references, version 1 has 31, and version 3 has 53. Again, there is a steady progression here in the number of references, typically indicating the ongoing evolution and the growing importance of the protocol.

The Initial NTP Proposal: RFC 958

When the initial NTP proposal was published in September 1985, the Internet was still a rather obscure phenomenon relegated to use by the academic communities, various national research centers, and the military. Also, it was only two years earlier, in January 1983, that the Internet began a conversion to TCP/IP protocols. The collective level of experience with TCP/IP, high-speed bandwidth, and large-size networks was minimal compared to what it is today. The thrust of RFC 958 was to advance the concept of NTP as a potential replacement for the Time Protocol (RFC 868) and the ICMP Timestamp messages as described in RFC 792, which specifies ICMP. RFC 958 specified only the NTP data representation and message formats but did not specify any of the synchronization algorithms or filtering mechanisms.

NTP Version 1: RFC 1059

The NTP version 1 specification that was published in July 1988 as RFC 1059 represents a significant enhancement over the initial NTP proposal. It describes the NTP architecture, algorithms, and protocols that are needed to synchronize local clocks in a distributed computing environment consisting of servers and clients. The NTP version 1 specification addressed the following key topics:

Description of the NTP service environment, which includes the implementation and service models. The implementation model as advanced in version 1 is the client/server model along with the consideration of a distributed hierarchy as a function of network complexity and size. The service model is based on the ability of the clients and servers to exchange updates that contain the necessary parameters to maintain synchronization. One of the derived values from the timestamps inside of an NTP message is called an *offset*. An offset is defined as the amount of time by which a local clock must be adjusted to bring it into correspondence with the clock source. Thus, an offset depends on the exchange of NTP updates via UDP, which itself does not guarantee reliable message delivery. That condition needs to be taken into account in the NTP service model.

Specification of NTP itself that includes data formats, state variables and parameters, the modes of NTP operation, and the processing of events. Data formats apply to the NTP state variables and parameters. State variable and parameters are categorized as follows:

- System variables that relate to the operating system environment and logical clock mechanisms

- Peer variables that are specific to each peer that's operating in a symmetric or client mode

- Packet variables that constitute the NTP message contents

- Parameters that are fixed in all implementations of a given NTP version

---

■**Note** For a complete list of NTP version 1 variables and parameters, the reader is referred directly to RFC 1059. The modes of NTP operation identified in RFC 1059 include client, server, and asymmetric. NTP events include peer timer expirations, arrival of NTP messages or detection of system faults, or operator commands.

Description of algorithms that include the clock filtering and selections algorithms. Both of these algorithms are intended to maintain the best possible level of time synchronization.

Description of logical clock design. A logical clock within NTP devices allows for periodic offset adjustments resulting from NTP calculations.

NTP Version 2: RFC 1119

NTP version 2 is significant in the sense that as of the time of writing it is the NTP version that retains the "standard" status. RFC 119 was published in September 1989.

Specific enhancements in version 2 over NTP version 1 include

- Increased support for operational modes that indicate the type of association that an NTP device is in or the type of association that it is willing to form. The mode field in the NTP message is used to indicate the mode type. The following modes are supported: symmetric active, symmetric passive, client, server, and broadcast.

- Support for NTP control messages that facilitate control and monitoring functions that might not be available via other network management tools.

- Support for cryptographic authentication that's based on the use of 64-bit Data Encryption Standard (DES) keys.

- Improved checks to avoid disruption due to unsynchronized, duplicate, or in some way invalid timestamps.

NTP Version 3: RFC 1305

RFC 1305 that specifies NTP version 3 was published in March 1992. The new specification neither alters the previous version in any major way nor obsoletes version 2 NTP implementations. However, the NTP version 3 algorithms take into account the increasing networking speeds (gigabit speeds were not mainstream in 1992, but they were already appearing on the networking horizons!) and incorporate enhancements to improve NTP accuracy and stability. Those enhancements include

- The overhaul of the local-clock algorithm. The new algorithm can result in lower NTP message rates, which implies less stress on the network bandwidth. The new algorithm allows for NTP interoperability with the previous versions.

- The introduction of a new algorithm for combining offsets from the peer timeservers. The new algorithm has been modeled after those that are used in the standards laboratories. The effect of the new algorithm is greater accuracy, stability, and fewer errors resulting from asymmetric paths between the peers across the Internet or networks where the potential for asymmetric communication exists.

- Minor changes to the local-clock algorithms to correct problems resulting from the leap second insertions into the UTC timescale.

- Changes to the definition, calculation, and processing of delay, offset, and dispersion with the goal of increasing the accuracy of the synchronization process.

More than a decade has passed, and the Internet has experienced a phenomenal explosion since the publication of RFC 1305. New challenges are facing the Internet community as a result of growth and threats. While work is continuing on NTP version 4 that addresses the issues of greater scalability and better security, it is still versions 2 and 3 and SNTP that represent the bulk of current deployment.

Secure NTP

Security provisions are optional in the RFC-based NTP implementations, including the now commonly deployed version 3. Any NTP implementation that includes authentication between NTP devices could thus qualify for the label that's occasionally used in network administration circles of "Secure NTP." However, no numbered RFC currently specifies "Secure NTP" explicitly even though an IETF draft on the subject of secure NTP was published in November 2002 (with an expiration date of May 2003) and a Secure Network Time Protocol IETF working group (stime) is in existence. The issue of enhancing the robustness of NTP security is receiving nonetheless very serious attention in the ongoing work on NTP version 4, as referenced in the subsequent "The Network Time Synchronization Project" section.

NTP version 3 security is based on private (as opposed to public) cryptography that involves predistributed certificates and keys. Whether public or private, cryptography is intended to protect against the modification of the NTP message data, which could result in the introduction of bogus timestamps and consequently the synchronization of devices to an erroneous time. The NTP version 2 and 3 security NTP itself does not provide for key distribution and management, which implies that this process must take place through other means. The lack of key management and the lack of support for public cryptography could potentially prove very unscalable in large NTP deployments.

Simple Network Time Protocol (SNTP)

SNTP—a simplified version of NTP—has undergone an evolution of its own. SNTP was initially defined in RFC 1361, was updated by RFC 1769, and was further updated by RFC 2030, which specified SNTP version 4. An RFC document that's intended to supersede RFC 2030 was published in April 2004, but it has not yet been assigned an RFC number.

The intent of SNTP is to provide a time synchronization protocol for environments where the demands for time accuracy are perhaps less stringent than those available through the complex and intricate algorithms of NTP. The net result is a less complex software with time synchronization functionality similar to NTP, as evidenced even through an identical SNTP/NTP version 4 message structure, but without the robustness of NTP's capabilities in terms of redundancy and accuracy. While the synchronization accuracies via NTP over the Internet (as opposed to a small dedicated network) may be on the order of low milliseconds, there are networking environments where accuracies on the order of fractions of seconds or even seconds are acceptable. SNTP is intended for those environments. SNTP is also intended for environments where time synchronization redundancy is less critical and a single stratum 1 server is deemed sufficient as opposed to having multiple stratum 1 servers peer with one another.

From a configuration perspective, it is recommended that SNTP clients be configured at the edges of the network (the highest stratum number) while an SNTP server be configured as a stratum 1 server. This recommendation translates into having intermediate NTP (not SNTP!) stratum servers where a multistratum deployment is deemed necessary. It also means that SNTP by itself—without the aid of NTP—is intended for flat deployments where the clients communicate directly with an SNTP server, as contrasted with larger hierarchical deployments where the NTP devices assume multiple roles of servers, clients, and peers and where the clients are configured with multiple servers. Unlike NTP clients, SNTP clients typically operate with a single SNTP server, which means no redundancy at the client level. However, given SNTP's multicast and anycast capabilities, the protocol is a strong candidate for networks where all of the clients can synchronize their time from a single server with minimal configuration effort on the part of a network administrator.

The additional capability within SNTP that's not available in NTP version 3 is the accommodation for IPv6 and Open System Interconnection (OSI) addressing.

The Network Time Synchronization Project

The NTP Synchronization project is spearheaded by David Mills of the University of Delaware with the participation of graduate students and volunteers. Funding for the project comes from such notables in the field of cutting-edge communications and space research as the Defense Advanced Research Projects Agency (DARPA), the National Science Foundation (NSF), Jet Propulsion Laboratories (JPL), the National Aeronautics and Space Administration (NASA), and the Navy Surface Weapons Center (NSWC).

The time synchronization project stems from a growing recognition that even though NTP version 3 and even some early deployments of version 4 (not standardized as of the time of this writing) may be adequate for many networking environments, the NTP that can scale across the Internet needs to be more robust. Two areas of great concern are

The need for autoconfiguration: Currently, the process of NTP configuration is manual, which makes it very unscalable in large and diverse networks. The lack of configuration scalability can become pronounced either during initial configuration or when NTP servers or primary clock sources become compromised because of damage, outright destruction, or prolonged communication links failures. See Chapter 5 for NTP configuration examples.

The need for scalable and secure authentication: Electronic warfare is a fact of life, and applications that are extremely time sensitive could be disrupted with the introduction of the wrong time into the network from unauthorized and bogus NTP servers. Authentication between clients and servers in mission-critical environments becomes essential. The security model that's part of the most commonly deployed version 3 does not scale well in large and diverse networks because of reliance on symmetric key cryptography with predistributed keys and certificates.

The time synchronization project is intended to address both issues of more robust autonomous configuration and security. In fact, the issues are closely coupled. The desirable outcome is an initial cryptographically secure clock source discovery and/or quick reconfiguration following a failure of network links and/or any NTP servers that are participating within the synchronization hierarchy.

The Interplanetary Internet

The Interplanetary Internet (IPN) is not exactly a reality yet, but neither is it science fiction. The IPN represents a very strong vision and is a subject of intense study among many scientists, engineers, programmers, space researchers, and explorers.

The Advanced Research Projects Agency (ARPA) that was hastily started in 1957 during the Eisenhower administration is credited with providing the impetus and the funding that led to the development of the Internet's ancestor, the ARPAnet. Over the years, ARPA has changed its name a few times back and forth between ARPA and DARPA (D=Defense). It's not surprising, however, that ARPA in its current incarnation as DARPA is funding Interplanetary Internet research as part of the Next Generation Internet Initiative. Plenty of challenges are staring IPN in the face, not the least of which is the issue of transmission delay (time!) associated with long distances between the planets in the solar system. But those issues are solvable, even if they do take some time.

Many lessons have already been learned from the operations of the earthly Internet. While flattening out the communication process and allowing communications to be almost instantaneous among participating devices (and the people behind them!), the current Internet is subject to a strict hierarchical structure in terms of routing and NTP deployment. Needless to say, time synchronization and accurate timekeeping will be of paramount importance in IPN in order to maintain the integrity of interplanetary communications. A new IPN version of NTP should be just a matter of time! Should those involved in the IPN project discover the means of transmitting information that is not subject to the speed of light limit, the issues associated with timekeeping and synchronization might get a significant boost. The invariance of the speed of light has revolutionized modern physics. Yet, scientific revelations preceded special relativity, and other groundbreaking discoveries have since followed. Exceeding the speed of light will not be easy. But no one should be surprised that it has already occurred, somewhere in time.

For more information online about the IPN, check out the following URLs:

- `http://computer.howstuffworks.com/interplanetary-internet.htm`

- `http://www.ipnsig.org/aboutstudy.htm`

CHAPTER 4

■■■

NTP Architecture

NTP operations fall broadly into the currently pervasive but hardly monolithic client/ server architectural model. Generically, the client/server model implies a distributed computing environment where devices cooperate through request/reply exchanges and the use of their individual processing power to achieve a specific application-level outcome. That outcome may be the selection of criteria-meeting records from a database, the routing of voice calls across an IP network, or, as in the case of NTP, the synchronization of time among the participating devices.

In the classic variant of the client/server model, clients make requests to servers that in turn oblige the requestors with the appropriate responses. Corresponding results follow. But what if clients can also assume the role of servers? What if servers can communicate as peers without restriction as to which server can initiate the communication process? And what if a hierarchy of servers has been configured to allow communication between them, but only with those immediately above or below in the hierarchical chain?

Certain NTP deployments (such as a single server that is synchronizing time for a small group of workstations) embody the classic elements of the client/server architecture. However, large implementations that involve numerous servers and possibly thousands of end-user devices are likely to complement the client/server model with elements of peer-to-peer processing where devices interact with one another as equal partners. Additionally, in large NTP deployments, the flow of communications between the servers follows a multitier hierarchy, with a potential for creating a distributed hierarchy as a function of redundancy/resiliency requirements. Thus, the NTP architecture is best described as being composite, since it lends itself to complex designs that involve peer-to-peer and/or client/server groups interacting in strictly hierarchical and/or hierarchically distributed computing environments.

A key to designing and/or identifying the NTP architecture for any given deployment lies in understanding the types of modes that NTP devices operate in and the subsequent associations they form between themselves.

NTP Servers, Clients, Hosts, and Peers

The expressions *server, client, host,* and *peer* could be applied to the same NTP device as a function of the mode in which the device operates and the spatial relationship of the observer to the device. Clients make requests, while servers respond to the client requests or advertise services without solicitation. With regard to peers and hosts, RFC 1305 (NTP version 3) adopts the terminology that a *host* refers to the instantiation of the NTP proto-col on the local processor, while a *peer* refers to the instantiation of the protocol on a remote processor that is connected to the host by a network path. From the perspective of a local NTP device making a request to synchronize its time with a remote NTP device, the labels applicable to the local device are *client* and *host*, while the labels that could be applied to the remote device are *server* and *peer*.

■**Note** NTP product vendors and/or implementers do not universally adhere to the terminology that's adopted in RFC 1305 in regard to NTP devices. For example, some vendors consider as NTP peers only those devices (typically servers) that are mutually willing to be synchronized. This terminology is in sync with the peer-to-peer computing model but not necessarily with the concept of an NTP peer as expressed in RFC 1305.

NTP Modes of Operation and Associations

The operational modes of NTP devices and the associations they form reflect the nature of interactions between them. For example, a host may offer synchronization services but not be willing to be synchronized by a peer. A host may offer synchronization serv-ices to multiple peers but not be willing to be synchronized by any of them. A host may request a synchronization service from a peer but not offer the service in return. A host may also offer a synchronization service to a peer and express a willingness to be syn-chronized by it. In practice, the NTP mode and association are not explicitly configurable but rather they result from the configuration of other parameters.

An NTP association is formed when two NTP-configured devices exchange messages and one or both of them create and maintain an instantiation of a protocol machine. Generically, an *instantiation* means the representation of an abstraction with a concrete example, while in the context of NTP associations an *instantiation* means the presence of an executable protocol machine. The concepts of a protocol machine, state machine, and finite state machine are expanded upon in the "Additional NTP Terms and Definitions" section of this chapter. Effectively, from a network administration perspective, an NTP association is formed when the functionality of NTP is activated through configuration, and subsequently messages are exchanged between NTP devices.

An NTP association may be of a very short duration, just long enough for a peer to respond to a message from a host. An association may also be ongoing and continue for as long as the device configuration does not change and network connectivity is maintained. The NTP mode and the type of association are represented by the value of the mode field in the NTP data message (see Chapter 3 for descriptions of NTP data message fields). The following modes have been specified in NTP version 3. The numbers in parentheses represent the corresponding value of the mode field in an NTP data message.

- Symmetric active (1)

- Symmetric passive (2)

- Client (3)

- Server (4)

- Broadcast (5)

Additionally, in NTP version 4 (still under specification as of the time of writing) and in version 4 of Simple Network Time Protocol (SNTP) as specified in RFC 2030, two additional modes have been defined:

- Multicast

- Manycast/anycast

The multicast and manycast/anycast modes are represented by values corresponding to the client, server, and broadcast modes in the mode field, along with IP addressing that transmits to a predefined multicast address or group. Consider now the characteristics of each NTP mode in more detail.

Symmetric Active Mode

A host that operates in the symmetric active mode sends periodic NTP data messages that announce its willingness to synchronize with and be synchronized by its peer(s). The messages are sent regardless of the reachability state or the stratum level of the peer(s). A typical scenario for the presence of the symmetric active mode is when two or more servers with the same stratum level peer with one another for the purpose of redundancy. The peering servers could be primary timeservers (stratum 1) that are equipped with reference clocks or stratum 2 servers that are synchronized with public stratum 1 servers over the Internet. Additionally, devices that are configured as local NTP "masters" and are not synchronized with UTC but instead rely on their local clocks also operate in a symmetric active mode with their peers. When a host has been configured as a local "master" with multiple peers, the configuration on the peers is limited to defining that host as their peer. The NTP data messages exchanged between that host and the peers would reflect the symmetric active mode.

■**Note** In the absence of a dedicated NTP timeserver that's synchronized with UTC via its own reference clock, any device (router, switch, workstation) that is configured as an NTP "master" can assume the role of a stratum 1 server and provide synchronization with a "relative" time that is typically determined and configured manually on the device by a network administrator. Although such a configuration provides synchronization, it does not provide an accurate UTC time.

The display in Listing 4-1 of truncated output from a debug ntp packets IOS command on a Cisco router (host), with an IP address of 192.168.3.1, illustrates the mode values of 1 in the NTP data packets being exchanged between this host and its peer. The IP address of the peer is 192.168.5.1.

Listing 4-1. *Output from* debug ntp packets *Command Illustrating NTP Symmetric Active Mode Exchanges with Mode 1 Values*

```
05:37:04: NTP: xmit packet to 192.168.5.1:
05:37:04:   leap 0, mode 1, version 3, stratum 1, ppoll 1024
.

05:38:06: NTP: rcv packet from 192.168.5.1 to 192.168.3.1 on Serial0:
05:38:06:   leap 0, mode 1, version 3, stratum 2, ppoll 64
.
```

In the preceding scenario, the initial messages that were exchanged immediately following the device configuration had mode values of 3 and 4 (client and server) as opposed to 1 (symmetric active). Only after the initial synchronization was achieved between the routers did both the host and its peer start to operate in the symmetric active mode with the mode value of 1.

Listing 4-2 illustrates the host (from the preceding scenario) operating in the symmetric active mode, while the peer is responding in a symmetric passive mode (mode value of 2). This condition is the result of removing the peer's running configuration file (via an IOS no command) of a statement that identified the host as its peer (no ntp peer 192.168.5.1). Following the reconfiguration, when the host (192.168.3.1) sends out an NTP data packet to 192.168.5.1, the mode value is 1, or symmetric active. When the host receives an NTP packet from 192.168.5.1, the mode value is 2, or symmetric passive.

Listing 4-2. *Output from* debug ntp packets *Command Illustrating Symmetric Passive NTP Mode Exchanges with Mode 1 and 2 Values*

```
05:08:14: NTP: xmit packet to 192.168.5.1:
05:08:14:   leap 0, mode 1, version 3, stratum 1, ppoll 1024
.

05:08:16: NTP: rcv packet from 192.168.5.1 to 192.168.3.1 on Serial0:
05:08:16:   leap 0, mode 2, version 3, stratum 2, ppoll 64
.
```

If, in the preceding scenario, the host and its peer were both defined as local "masters," in addition to each one identifying the other as its peer, they both would continue to operate in the symmetric active mode, similarly to a configuration where only the host is defined as a master clock. In practice, when multiple NTP devices are configured as local "masters," and each one defines the others as peers, the scenario is representative of a redundant NTP server configuration. The "master" devices could be acting as servers to numerous clients while peering with one another to maintain synchronization among themselves. Figure 4-1 illustrates a typical scenario where NTP devices are operating in symmetric active mode. The devices that are identified in Figure 4-1 as NTP Server 1, NTP Server 2, and NTP Server 3 could be dedicated primary timeservers, routers, switches, Unix/Linux servers, Novell servers, or a combination of any of the preceding NTP servers. In practice, the devices would be configured at the same stratum level.

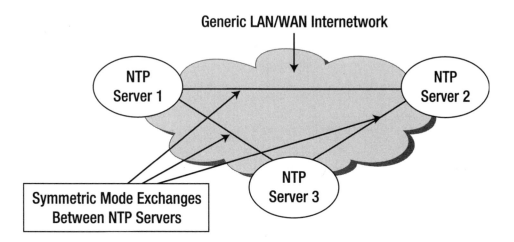

Figure 4-1. *Redundant NTP servers operating in a symmetric active mode*

■**Caution** Note that when multiple Cisco devices are configured as the local "masters," there will be an initial delay in time synchronization (30+ minutes) if the time on the devices is set to different values. Synchronization will nonetheless occur as long as the devices have been configured at different stratum levels. Otherwise, if multiple "master" devices are configured with the same stratum number, experience and experiments dictate that synchronization may never take place between them, thus leaving NTP in an unstable state throughout the network.

Symmetric Passive Mode

The symmetric passive mode is closely coupled with the operations of the symmetric active mode. When a host operates in a symmetric active mode and its peer has been identified through configuration, then under certain operational conditions (removal of the peer configuration statement on the peer) the peer is going to respond to the host in a symmetric passive mode, expressing its willingness to be synchronized. Consider the symmetric passive mode and type of association as being in response to changing the configuration rather than as a result of any initial configuration.

According to RFC 1305, the symmetric passive mode association is likely to be more transient than the symmetric active mode one. However, practical experience dictates that in the Cisco router environment a symmetric passive mode association may persist (even if a corresponding symmetric active association has been dissolved) until a device that has created that association has been rebooted. While RFC 1305 represents a specification, some details of the implementation of the specification are likely to vary between vendors.

Client Mode

The client and server modes are closely coupled in a manner similar to the symmetric active and passive modes. By operating in a client mode, a host expresses a willingness to be synchronized by a peer but not to synchronize the peer. A host that is operating in a client mode sends periodic messages to the peer (configured as a server on the host) regardless of the reachability status or stratum level of the peer.

A typical device operating as an NTP client could be a LAN workstation. However, edge routers and switches in a layered internetwork can readily assume the roles of NTP clients. It is entirely possible that the edge routers and switches, while configured as clients to one or more servers that are located closer to the core of the network, could also be acting as servers to end-user LAN workstations.

In a Cisco router environment, when a host defines a peer as a server through configuration, the host is going to operate in the client mode, while the peer will operate in the server mode. Listing 4-3 and Listing 4-4 resulting from the IOS debug ntp packets command on a host router illustrate an exchange (one transmit and one receive message)

between the client (host) and its peer that the client has defined as a server via an ntp
server 192.168.3.1 command. The host's IP is 192.168.5.1.

Listing 4-3. *Transmit Message from Host (Client) to Peer (Server) Illustrating Mode 3 Value*

```
00:16:29: NTP: xmit packet to 192.168.3.1:
00:16:29:  leap 0, mode 3, version 3, stratum 2, ppoll 64
00:16:29:  rtdel 0269 (9.415), rtdsp 0017 (0.351), refid C0A80301 (192.168.3.1)
00:16:29:  ref C64D5CFD.92022E07 (11:14:05.570 UTC Sun Jun 5 2005)
00:16:29:  org C64D5CFD.90C83E6F (11:14:05.565 UTC Sun Jun 5 2005)
00:16:29:  rec C64D5CFD.92022E07 (11:14:05.570 UTC Sun Jun 5 2005)
00:16:29:  xmt C64D5CFE.876D81D6 (11:14:06.529 UTC Sun Jun 5 2005)
```


Listing 4-4. *Receive Message from Peer (Server) to Host (Client) Illustrating Mode 4 Value*

```
00:16:29: NTP: rcv packet from 192.168.3.1 to 192.168.5.1 on Serial1:
00:16:29:  leap 0, mode 4, version 3, stratum 1, ppoll 64
00:16:29:  rtdel 0000 (0.000), rtdsp 0002 (0.031), refid 4C4F434C (76.79.67.76)
00:16:29:  ref C64D5CD7.E9A06BB2 (11:13:27.912 UTC Sun Jun 5 2005)
00:16:30:  org C64D5CFE.876D81D6 (11:14:06.529 UTC Sun Jun 5 2005)
00:16:30:  rec C64D5CFE.88A3FF82 (11:14:06.533 UTC Sun Jun 5 2005)
00:16:30:  xmt C64D5CFE.90CE2339 (11:14:06.565 UTC Sun Jun 5 2005)
00:16:30:  inp C64D5CFE.9202BEBB (11:14:06.570 UTC Sun Jun 5 2005)
```

Note that the timestamps in the messages reflect synchronization, which occurred
within seconds of configuration. On the host (client), the time prior to configuration—and
subsequent synchronization—was more than a month off from that on the peer (server).

Server Mode

The server mode and association are established in response to requests from clients.
This mode and association reflect the willingness of the device to offer synchronization
services to the clients but not to be synchronized by them. The server association does
not persist past the response to the client; i.e., the server maintains no state information
about the client. On a Cisco router (host) that's defined as a "master," and with a peer
defining this router as a server, the transmissions to the peer are stateless, as reflected
in Listing 4-5.

Listing 4-5. *Output from* debug ntp packets *Command Illustrating a Stateless Transmission from a Server*

```
01:10:28: NTP: stateless xmit packet to 192.168.5.1:
01:10:28:   leap 0, mode 4, version 3, stratum 4, ppoll 64
01:10:28:   rtdel 0000 (0.000), rtdsp 0002 (0.031), refid 7F7F0701 (127.127.7.1)
01:10:28:   ref C64D6957.E993473D (12:06:47.912 UTC Sun Jun 5 2005)
01:10:28:   org C64D6966.8C526210 (12:07:02.548 UTC Sun Jun 5 2005)
01:10:28:   rec C64D6966.8E23EA55 (12:07:02.555 UTC Sun Jun 5 2005)
01:10:28:   xmt C64D6966.9601E6F4 (12:07:02.585 UTC Sun Jun 5 2005)
```

The output from the show ntp associations command on the host (server) that makes the stateless transmissions confirms that there is no association for its interactions with the client device, as shown in Listing 4-6.

Listing 4-6. *Output from* show ntp associations *Command Illustrating on a Server the Absence of an Association with a Client*

```
Router2#show ntp associations
          address       ref clock    st  when    poll   reach  delay offset disp
*~127.127.7.1  76.79.67.76    3      51      64     377    0.0   0.00   0.0
* master (synced), # master (unsynced), + selected, - candidate, ~ configured
Router2#
```

The existing association on the server results from the server being configured as the "master." In contrast, the association on the client machine persists with respect to the server, as depicted in Listing 4-7.

Listing 4-7. *Output from* show ntp associations *Command on a Client Illustrating an Association with a Server*

```
Router4#show ntp associations
          address       ref clock    st  when    poll   reach delay offset  disp
*~192.168.3.1  127.127.7.1    4       6      64     377    9.2   2.03   0.1
 * master (synced), # master (unsynced), + selected, - candidate, ~ configured
Router4#
```

The IP address of 192.168.3.1 has been assigned to a physical interface on the server. The codes in front of the address reflect that the client considers the server as the master and is synchronized to it. The "ref clock" value of 127.127.7.1 represents the IP address of the reference clock for this client. See the entry "Reference clock IP addressing" in the section "Additional NTP Terms and Definitions" later in this chapter for an explanation of the reference clock IP address format.

Broadcast Mode

An NTP host that operates in the broadcast mode sends out periodic messages that announce the willingness of the host to synchronize all of the receiving hosts, but not be synchronized by them. The truncated display in Listing 4-8 shows the output from the IOS debug ntp packets command for a Cisco router host operating in the broadcast mode.

Listing 4-8. *Output from* debug ntp packets *Command Illustrating Broadcast NTP Mode with a Mode 5 Value*

```
06:20:25: NTP: xmit packet to 255.255.255.255:
06:20:25:  leap 0, mode 5, version 3, stratum 4, ppoll 64
.
```

Note that the NTP packet is transmitted to a local broadcast address of 255.255.255.255, which means this packet is not going to leave the local subnet, as routers do not forward local broadcasts. This is unless, of course, a router that is interfaced to the local subnet supports the feature of listening to NTP broadcasts and is specifically configured to forward them. In practice, however, if an NTP server is configured to operate in the broadcast mode, it is likely to be positioned on the edge of a network making broadcast transmissions to end-user workstations. If an NTP broadcast server is servicing network infrastructure components such as routers or switches, those devices would have to be within reach of broadcast traffic, i.e., part of the same subnet as the broadcast server. This is unless, of course, directed broadcast configuration becomes a feature of NTP, which would allow broadcasting from a server to specific subnets. As a function of vendor implementations for a multihomed NTP server—especially in the case of routers with multiple interfaces— NTP servers may be user configurable to broadcast on specific rather than all interfaces. This feature offers granularity and flexibility in NTP configuration and administration.

Multicast Mode

The multicast mode is available in SNTP and is also a part of the evolving NTP version 4 specification. A multicast server sends out periodic messages to the NTP multicast group class D IP address, which has been assigned the value of 224.0.1.1 by the Internet Assigned Numbers Authority (IANA). NTP clients must be configured to listen to the unsolicited multicast messages from the servers, but the clients do not have to respond to the servers in order to become synchronized. However, a client receiving a multicast message from a server may send a unicast message to the server to determine the round-trip delay between them.

Note The round-trip delay, which is one of the variables that's used in the NTP clock-filter procedure, is derived from the four timestamps inside of an NTP data message (see Chapter 3 for descriptions of NTP data message contents). One of the functions of the clock-filter procedure is to select the best offset samples from a given clock. An *offset* represents the amount of time by which a local clock needs to be adjusted in order to bring it into conformance with a reference clock.

Unless the multicast clients reside on the same subnet as the multicast server, consideration must also be given to the routing of multicast traffic between the relevant subnets. When clients are separated from servers by one or more routers, they must implement a multicast management protocol, such as the Internet Group Management Protocol (IGMP), in order for routers to join the multicast group and pass the multicast traffic between the subnets.

Note IGMP version 3 is specified in the standards track category in RFC 3376. The IANA Considerations for IPv4 IGMP are addressed in the best current practice category in RFC 3228.

Security is also a key consideration for the multicast mode deployments. Since all of the SNTP or NTP servers that operate in the multicast mode use the same multicast group address (224.0.1.1), there is always the potential for a rogue or misconfigured multicast server to disrupt the synchronization of the clients. Network administrators ought to consider taking all of the necessary and available security precautions to minimize the potential of NTP synchronization disruption. Implementing access control that is based on the trusted server's IP address is one option. Additionally, where the vendor implementation supports it, consider the configuration cryptographic NTP authentication. See the "NTP Security Considerations" section later in this chapter.

Manycast/Anycast Mode

Similarly to the multicast mode, the manycast/anycast mode is a feature of SNTP and the evolving NTP version 4. The SNTP specification (RFC 2030) refers to this mode as *anycast*. NTP version 4 notes refer to this mode as *manycast*. NTP vendors seem to make no distinction between the expressions. For the purpose of this work, the two expressions are considered synonymous and may be used interchangeably.

The anycast mode allows NTP clients to send time synchronization requests to a designated multicast address (224.0.1.1). In turn, servers that have been configured for the anycast mode respond to the client requests with unicast messages. A unicast reply from a server to a client, following a multicast request from a client, implies that both the server and the client now know each other's IP addresses. Clients then form associations with the servers that respond first, ignoring responses from other servers. The subsequent traffic between the clients and servers is unicast, falling into the point-to-point NTP mode category.

From the network administration perspective, the advantage of the anycast mode is that clients do not have to be preconfigured with the IP addresses of the servers in order to obtain the NTP synchronization service. However, the routing of multicast traffic must be supported between the clients and servers, unless all of them are part of the same subnet. An additional network administration consideration for the anycast and multicast modes is the isolation of the multicast traffic only to the required subnets rather than allowing its propagation throughout the entire network.

The practice of limiting the propagation of multicast traffic to a designated domain may take the form of the following:

Adjusting the Time to Live (TTL) counter in the IP header of the multicast messages to a value that predetermines the maximum number of hops (routers) that the messages will go through. The TTL field can assume a maximum value of 255. Should the value of TTL for originating multicast messages be left at 0, it means that the messages could go through hundreds of routers (and subnets) before reaching the maximum value of 255 and being discarded.

Enabling multicast routing in a very selective manner, only where it is required for NTP operations, rather than throughout the whole network.

Some installations, of course, may not view the NTP multicast traffic as a sufficient enough burden upon the computational network resources in order to allocate the necessary human resources for a proper multicast network design.

NTP Mode Categories

Collectively, the NTP modes fall into three categories, as summarized in Table 4-1.

Table 4-1. *NTP Mode Categories*

Mode Category	Mode
Point-to-point	Symmetric active
	Symmetric passive
	Client
	Server
Point-to-multipoint	Broadcast
	Multicast
Multipoint-to-point	Manycast/anycast

Out of the three NTP mode categories, the NTP devices that operate in any of the point-to-point modes—which are also referred to as the *unicast modes*—will require the maximum level of configuration. This means that the IP addresses of the communicating NTP devices have to be explicitly identified in the device configuration files, which potentially makes the configuration process unscalable in very large deployments. Lack of configuration scalability often leads to misconfigurations and a subsequent lack of time synchronization and/or the appearance of erroneous timestamps throughout a network. However, to support NTP unicast mode operations, there are no additional routing configuration requirements beyond what's already needed for any other unicast IP traffic.

The availability of the point-to-multipoint and the multipoint-to-point modes eases the NTP configuration and scalability burden. However, these modes require network administrators to ensure that multicast routing is properly supported and enabled and that NTP broadcast traffic is localized to the directly connected subnets or routers are configured to selectively forward it to intended destinations.

NTP Variables and Procedures

Many algorithms or procedures undergird the time synchronization process among NTP devices. They include clock-update, primary-clock, transmit, receive, packet, clear, poll-update, clock-filter, clock-selection, and multiple initialization procedures. While the developers of NTP products need to be familiar with the inner workings of these procedures, network administrators who are responsible for configuring and troubleshooting NTP deployments are mostly interested in the variables (and their values) that are employed in those procedures.

NTP Variables Classes

The dozens of variables from NTP procedures have been categorized into classes, as outlined in Table 4-2.

Table 4-2. *NTP Variables' Classes*

Variable Class	Description
System variables	Variables that relate to the OS environment and local-clock mechanism
Peer variables	Variables that represent the state of the protocol machine that is specific to each peer
Packet variables	Variables that are part of the NTP messages
Parameters	Constants for all implementations of the current NTP version

When the same variables are included in two or more of the classes from Table 4-2, they are referred to as the *common variables*. For example, the poll interval, precision, root delay, and root dispersion are variables common to the system, peer, and packet classes. To differentiate the same common variables from different classes, a prefix is added to identify the class in the variable name; i.e., sys.rootdelay, peer.rootdelay, and pkt.rootdelay represent the rootdelay common variable from the system, peer, and packet classes, respectively.

The variables that are configurable or that can be viewed through the various NTP utilities, debug, and display commands during troubleshooting are of greatest importance to the administrators. It should be noted, however, that different vendors may use their own unique mnemonics to describe NTP outputs resulting from their own display and troubleshooting commands. A specific vendor's NTP documentation should always be consulted to determine the exact meaning of what's displayed in the output and whether it corresponds to a specific NTP variable or represents a derived quantity.

Sample Analysis of NTP Variables

For the purpose of analysis of NTP variables, consider the following four sample outputs (Listings 4-9 through 4-12) from the show ntp associations detail command on a Cisco router that has been configured as a client of a "master" (another Cisco router) operating at stratum 2. The first output, in Listing 4-9, shows the client synchronized with the master clock at an approximate time of 18:08:25 10 Jul 1994. In the second output, in Listing 4-10, the client is no longer synchronized after the time on the master was advanced by ten-plus years (to the time of 14:00:00 11 May 2005). The client now considers the master as insane and its time as invalid. In the third output, in Listing 4-11, the client is still attempting to synchronize its time with the master clock after the timestamps have been reset to zero, or 00:00:00 January 1, 1900. Note that the client still considers the master as insane and its time as invalid. In the fourth and final output, in Listing 4-12, the client has synchronized its time with the master once again and considers the master as sane and its time as valid. The lesson here for administrators is that time synchronization takes time (minutes in the forthcoming analysis) during which the time on the client may be bogus.

Listing 4-9. *First Output from NTP Variables' Analysis (Client and Server Are Synchronized)*

```
Router2#show ntp associations detail
192.168.5.1 configured, our_master, sane, valid, stratum 2
ref ID 127.127.7.1, time B1CAB73F.9919F4A8 (18:06:55.598 UTC Sun Jul 10 1994)
our mode active, peer mode passive, our poll intvl 64, peer poll intvl 64
root delay 0.00 msec, root disp 0.03, reach 377, sync dist 4.684
delay 9.25 msec, offset -2.1989 msec, dispersion 0.03
precision 2**19, version 3
org time B1CAB774.33A6EA5A (18:07:48.201 UTC Sun Jul 10 1994)
rcv time B1CAB774.3566828A (18:07:48.208 UTC Sun Jul 10 1994)
xmt time B1CAB774.32CE329D (18:07:48.198 UTC Sun Jul 10 1994)
filtdelay =   9.25  9.00  9.20  9.20  9.19  9.14  9.14  9.00
filtoffset = -2.20 -2.20 -2.17 -2.16 -2.18 -2.06 -2.04 -1.97
filterror =   0.02  0.99  1.97  2.94  3.92  4.90  5.87  6.85
```

Listing 4-10. *Second Output for NTP Variables' Analysis (Time on the Master Advanced by Ten-Plus Years)*

```
Router2#show ntp associations detail
192.168.5.1 configured, insane, invalid, stratum 2
ref ID 127.127.7.1, time C62C8E90.291E2CBB (14:00:48.160 UTC Wed May 11 2005)
our mode active, peer mode passive, our poll intvl 64, peer poll intvl 64
root delay 0.00 msec, root disp 15875.03, reach 375, sync dist 31754.623
delay 9.16 msec, offset 341956304561.8464 msec, dispersion 15875.02
precision 2**19, version 3
org time C62C8EC4.C3C46E6C (14:01:40.764 UTC Wed May 11 2005)
rcv time B1CAB7F4.351B723B (18:09:56.207 UTC Sun Jul 10 1994)
xmt time B1CAB7F4.329E52B6 (18:09:56.197 UTC Sun Jul 10 1994)
filtdelay =      9.16  9.25  9.00  9.20  9.20  9.19  9.14  9.14
filtoffset = 3419563 -2.20 -2.20 -2.17 -2.16 -2.18 -2.06 -2.04
filterror =      0.02  1.97  2.94  3.92  4.90  5.87  6.85  7.83
```

Listing 4-11. *Third Output for NTP Variables' Analysis (No Synchronization Still Between Client and Master, and Timestamps Reset to Zero)*

```
Router2#show ntp associations detail
192.168.5.1 configured, insane, invalid, stratum 2
ref ID 127.127.7.1, time C62C8F60.5C530E4A (14:04:16.360 UTC Wed May 11 2005)
our mode active, peer mode passive, our poll intvl 64, peer poll intvl 64
root delay 0.00 msec, root disp 875.03, reach 0, sync dist 1755.127
delay 8.94 msec, offset 341956245574.0422 msec, dispersion 16000.00
precision 2**19, version 3
org time 00000000.00000000 (00:00:00.000 UTC Mon Jan 1 1900)
rcv time 00000000.00000000 (00:00:00.000 UTC Mon Jan 1 1900)
xmt time 00000000.00000000 (00:00:00.000 UTC Mon Jan 1 1900)
filtdelay =  0.00    0.00    0.00    0.00    0.00    0.00    0.00    0.00
filtoffset = 0.00    0.00    0.00    0.00    0.00    0.00    0.00    0.00
filterror = 16000.0 16000.0 16000.0 16000.0 16000.0 16000.0 16000.0 16000.0
```

Listing 4-12. *Fourth Output for NTP Variables' Analysis (Client and Master Are Again Synchronized)*

```
Router2#show ntp associations detail
192.168.5.1 configured, our_master, sane, valid, stratum 2
ref ID 127.127.7.1, time C62C90A0.5C553709 (14:09:36.360 UTC Wed May 11 2005)
our mode active, peer mode passive, our poll intvl 64, peer poll intvl 64
root delay 0.00 msec, root disp 0.03, reach 37, sync dist 879.974
delay 9.20 msec, offset -0.5576 msec, dispersion 875.35
precision 2**19, version 3
org time C62C90AF.4B5DD083 (14:09:51.294 UTC Wed May 11 2005)
rcv time C62C90AF.4CB0548F (14:09:51.299 UTC Wed May 11 2005)
xmt time C62C90AF.4A1B1ADE (14:09:51.289 UTC Wed May 11 2005)
filtdelay =   9.20 11.61  9.02  9.23  9.14    0.00    0.00    0.00
filtoffset = -0.56  0.62 -0.60 -0.68 -0.39    0.00    0.00    0.00
filterror =   0.02  0.99  1.97  2.94  3.92 16000.0 16000.0 16000.0
```

Information in the preceding outputs, in Listing 4-9 through Listing 4-12, is derived from the state of select NTP variables and the ongoing results of NTP data and control messages exchanges between the client and the server. In the course of the messages exchanges, the NTP packet procedure executes a series of tests that are commonly referred to as *sanity checks*, the results of which are also reflected in the outputs. Thus, while the outputs display directly the values of some variables, as a whole, and by applying algorithms to the ongoing exchanges, they present a more composite and meaningful picture of the state of an NTP association than a mere raw data dump of all the available variables. The outputs include

- **Values of select NTP variables**: Those values are being displayed in near real time, i.e., since the last update following an exchange between this host and its peer. They include the poll intervals, root and peer dispersions, and timestamps.

- **A mini-history of changes in the values of select variables as a function of time**: This running mini-history is from the last eight exchanges between this host and its peer (last three lines of each output). It displays the values of the round-trip delays, offsets, and approximate errors for each sample, which are represented, respectively, by the filtdelay, filtoffset, and filterror descriptors.

- **Results of sanity checks**: The results the NTP sanity checks are displayed on the first lines of the outputs.

NTP Sanity Checks

The results from the sanity checks are depicted as sane/insane for the peer and valid/invalid for the time. Initially (the first output in Listing 4-9, which is ground zero for the purpose of this analysis), the client considered the server as sane and its time as valid. In the second output (Listing 4-10), following a time reset on the master of ten-plus years ahead, the client considered the peer as insane and its time as invalid or not believable. Following a series of exchanges that lasted for several minutes, the client still considered the master as insane and its time as invalid (third output, Listing 4-11) but for a different reason. The timestamps were now reset to zero. In the fourth output (Listing 4-12), the client once again synchronized its time to that of the server.

RFC 1305 identifies eight tests relating to the NTP message header and data validity, as listed in Table 4-3. These checks are responsible for the client declaring the master as sane or insane and its time as valid or invalid.

Table 4-3. *NTP Tests (Sanity Checks)*

Test #	Test Description
1	Transmit timestamp must not match the last one received from the same peer.
2	Originate timestamp matches the last one sent to the same peer.
3	Both originate and receive timestamps must be nonzero.
4	Calculated delay must be within "reasonable" bounds.
5	Authentication needs to be disabled, or the authenticator must be present and correct as determined by the decrypt procedure.
6	The peer clock must be synchronized and the interval (since the peer clock was last updated) must be positive and less than an NTP parameter max clock age represented as NTP.MAXAGE.
7	Host will not synchronize on a peer with a greater stratum.
8	The NTP message header needs to contain "reasonable" values for the pkt.rootdelay and pkt.rootdispersion variables.

Note the high value of root dispersion (15875.03) in the second output when the client declared the server as insane, and compare this value with that from the first output. Test 8 relates to a "reasonable" value of pkt.rootdispersion. When the client declared the server as insane in the third output, note that values of time originate and transmit timestamps were both zero, which is what test 3 checks.

Configurable Variables

Very few NTP variables are configurable. This statement applies not only to the variables that appear in Listing 4-9 through Listing 4-12 but also in general. The IP address of the peer that appears on the first line of the outputs in Listing 4-9 through Listing 4-12 is one example of a configurable variable. Stratum level is also configurable, and it was configured on the server (peer) to the value of 2. Past these two variables, no other ones appearing in the four outputs are directly configurable. The modes are indirectly configurable, as their values are a function of certain configuration commands and keywords (server, peer, broadcast, multicast).

The "configured" descriptor that follows the IP address simply indicates that the peer IP was configured statistically rather than being dynamically discovered and is thus a reflection of the peer IP address configuration. The "our_master" descriptor in the first and fourth outputs indicates that this host (local machine) is synchronized to the peer, thus reflecting a state between the machines. Note that there is no "our_master" descriptor in the second and third outputs, as the client was not synchronized to its peer.

The "ref ID" represents the IP address of the machine to which the peer (server) is synchronized. The value of 127.127.7.1 for the "ref ID" represents a class A loopback address, or an address that is internal to the peer and could not appear as an external destination in the network routing tables. This means that the peer is not synchronized to another external NTP server and uses its local clock as the time source.

The particular "ref ID" IP address in the outputs was not configured but rather pre-determined by default by the IOS. However, in a different scenario with more servers, the "ref ID" IP could be represented as an IP value of a peer of this server and technically be configurable. The "time" following the "ref ID" represents the last timestamp that the peer received from its master, or, in this case, its local clock. By configuring the server as the master clock and setting its time, the administrator did exercise an indirect control over this time value.

Nonconfigurable Variables

In Listing 4-9 through Listing 4-12, the poll intervals (our poll intvl and peer poll intvl), the root delay, the root dispersion (root disp), the round-trip delay to the peer (delay), the offset between this host and the peer (offset), and the dispersion of the peer clock (dispersion) are all examples of nonconfigurable NTP variables. Even though administrators have no control over these variables, viewing their values is useful in troubleshooting.

Consider, for example, the value of offset 341956304561.8464 ms for the offset in Listing 4-10. A conversion from milliseconds into days yields the value of approximately 3,958 days, or more than 10 years' difference between the clock values, which is a clear example of the lack of synchronization. In contrast, the offset from Listing 4-12 is a fraction of a millisecond, reflecting a good potential for synchronization, which is confirmed by other elements of that output.

NTP Security Considerations

NTP security features are best examined in the context of the overall security framework that considers the following elements for each NTP deployment:

NTP-inherent security features: NTP comes equipped with several methods of cryptographic authentication, which vary as a function of the NTP version. Version 3 supports the symmetric private key cryptography, while version 4 supports both, the symmetric private key cryptography and the Autokey protocol. The Autokey protocol allows for cryptographic authentication that is based on public keys.

Operating system security: The various operating systems that support the NTP application (numerous flavors of Unix [OpenBSD, Solaris, AIX, FreeBSD, HP-UX], Cisco IOS, Juniper JUNOS, Novell NetWare, various versions of Microsoft Windows, Linux, and more) normally offer security for all of their applications via varying levels of access control mechanisms, thus allowing the NTP operations to take advantage of those OS-based security implementations.

Network infrastructure security: The networks over which NTP operates are likely to implement parameter and internal security that includes firewalls, a degree of intrusion detection and/or prevention, physical security, and operational procedures that will be (or at least should be!) driven by a well-defined security policy.

The preceding components of an NTP security framework are closely coupled, and they all need to be taken into account during NTP deployments. While a detailed discussion of network security is not congruent with the intent of this publication, there are generic security considerations that apply equally to the network infrastructure, a specific network component or platform, or a singular application such as NTP. Those considerations can be reduced to the following:

Threat identification: Potential security threats against the network, a specific network component, or an application such as NTP must be clearly identified. Security threats include but are not limited to information disclosure, information corruption, and denial of service (DoS). Security breaches due to those threats are often facilitated by ineffective implementation of authentication and authorization features.

Risk analysis: Risk analysis leads to a decision regarding whether it is desirable to protect an entire network, any of its components, or a specific application against the identified threats via any of the available security antidotes. Security antidotes enforce information confidentiality (protection against disclosures of sensitive content), information integrity (protection against data corruption including alteration), and network/system availability (protection against DoS attacks). In case a decision is made to protect the network, any of its components, or a specific application against the identified threats, the degree and the cost of protection should be considered against the potential cost of loss resulting from a security breach.

Resource allocation: Resource allocation and implementation planning of the security antidotes come next, in the event that the analysis leads to a decision to deploy them against the identified threats.

Monitoring: Ongoing monitoring and periodic security audits improve the overall effectiveness of the implementation by increasing the potential for catching and addressing any emerging threats.

The bottom-line question that needs to be answered with regard to NTP security is, what is the value to the business or an institution of having a synchronized and accurate time across the network? Or, conversely, what is the impact of having a synchronized but an inaccurate time? Or, what is the impact of having an unsynchronized time across the network, with some of the devices being very close to an accurate UTC time while others ticking quite a bit off that standard? Those questions also get to the very heart of the reason for NTP deployment in the first place. Answering those questions and applying the preceding generic security considerations to a potential NTP deployment should enable network administrators to determine how best to secure NTP. However, regardless of whether or not those questions can be answered satisfactorily or the preceding generic security considerations applied successfully, the mere fact that NTP is being deployed is an indication that a value has been placed on accurate and/or synchronized timekeeping. In all likelihood, that value will then drive the implementation of the available security antidotes to secure the NTP deployment.

NTP Access Control

Implementation of NTP access control will determine who will communicate with whom, at what level of service, and/or who will trust whom when advertising NTP services. NTP clients (remember that NTP devices can wear multiple hats; i.e., a device may act as a client with respect to a certain server but also act as a server with respect to other devices!) could be configured to accept some or all of the services from one or more servers or, conversely, to access only select services on a specific server or group.

The typical filtering mechanisms for NTP access control are IP addresses, the type of NTP service being offered or requested, and the direction of communication. For example, access control could allow a device to send time requests but not NTP control query requests. Or, access control could allow the sending of control query requests without allowing the requestor to synchronize its time with the server to which the query requests are being sent. Access control could also result in the rejection of time or control query requests from all or some of the requestors. See Chapter 5 for examples of access control configurations.

The enabling and disabling of NTP broadcasts via a specific interface also falls under the umbrella of access control, even though no IP addresses or specific services are identified in those configurations statements. The level of granularity in access control will vary between vendors and as a function of the type of devices on which NTP is implemented. For example, the operating systems on Cisco, Juniper, or Nortel routers and switches all have extensive access control capabilities that can be employed in support of NTP security. In contrast, operating systems for end-user devices offer minimal if any access control support.

In the context of implementing antidotes against the security threats of disclosure, corruption, and DoS, the role of access control is to minimize the potential for NTP data corruption by restricting the flow of communication and services to specific devices. But, while the role of access control is important, it is well understood among network security personnel that it must be complemented with other security measures in order to be fully effective.

If the communicating NTP devices themselves are vulnerable and open to intruder penetration because of poor device-level access control, operating system bugs that can be exploited to provide access to the devices by unauthorized personnel, inadequate physical security, and/or lack of adherence to security procedures by the device operators and users, then no amount of NTP access control configuration is going to prevent a determined intruder from gaining access to those devices. Additionally, even if NTP access control is configured but the NTP data and control messages are being transmitted in the clear, the potential always exists for the interception and alteration of the message contents. The end result of the preceding is compromised timekeeping across the network.

NTP Cryptographic Authentication

Cryptographic authentication is a strong security mechanism for enforcing NTP data integrity. When it is configured to authenticate the NTP messages exchanges and the resulting associations, it raises the bar for would-be intruders attempting to disrupt synchronization and/or accurate timekeeping on the network.

Cryptographic authentication in NTP does not ensure data confidentiality. Authentication is not encryption. A potential intruder could still intercept the NTP messages, view their contents, and replay them at a later time either unchanged or modified. However, the NTP peers for whom the messages were intended would be able to detect that the messages were modified and consequently reject them. After all, the correct UTC time is not a big secret that must be carefully guarded from intruders, but depriving intruders of the ability to alter the correct time on critical network devices can prevent big problems! On the other hand, there might be those unique NTP deployments where an incorrect but synchronized time on a network is intentional, in which case preventing potential intruders from viewing NTP messages might assume greater importance.

Effectively, cryptographic authentication allows hosts to trust their peers and consider them as legitimate rather than as deliberate or accidental intruders. While the cryptographic authentication process is deemed to be very secure, poor key management procedures and/or the lack of scalability in key distribution could compromise and diminish the value of this security antidote. Keys falling into the hands of intruders would allow them to pose as legitimate NTP servers and mount a variety of attacks. And the inability to distribute keys securely and in a scalable manner negates the very value of having the cryptographic authentication feature available within NTP.

The symmetric (private) key cryptography is an optional feature in NTPv3, but most vendors implement it. The evolving NTPv4 also supports the private key cryptography in addition to offering an even more robust security via the Autokey protocol.

Symmetric Key Cryptography

The initial implementations of the symmetric key cryptography in NTP version 3 (specified in RFC 1305 in 1992!) were based on the Cyber Block Chaining (CBC) operation mode of the Data Encryption Standard (DES). The DES-CBC produces a one-way hash (a message digest) that can be used to verify the identity of an NTP peer. The DES-CBC method has been subsequently replaced with the Message Digest 5 (MD5) algorithm, which was developed by Ronald L. Rivest and described in RFC 1321.

■**Note** The essence of the one-way hash or message digest functions is that they produce a fixed-length output based on arbitrary-length input. The reason for the "one-way" modifier is that it is practically impossible (although not theoretically impossible!) to figure out the input based on the output. Good one-way message digest functions possess certain common characteristics. Given a significant random sample of inputs, any particular bit in the resulting outputs should be on about half of the time, each output should have about half of its bits on, and for inputs that are extremely similar (literally one or two bits off!) the outputs should bear no correlation to one another.

From the configuration perspective, the symmetric MD5 key cryptography requires that the communicating NTP devices be configured with the same key and key identifier, or key ID. Both NTP versions 3 and 4 use a 128-bit key and a 32-bit key ID. The configuration of the NTP symmetric cryptography thus sounds simple enough, as long as a mechanism is in place for key management. In order for the private key cryptographic configuration to be effective and not simply offer a sense of false security to the administrators, keys must be delivered securely to each participating device and subsequently be stored securely either in a key file or directly in the device configuration statements.

The crux of the problem with key distribution in private key cryptography is that in order to securely transmit a secret key over an insecure network, the key must be encrypted. And in order to encrypt a secret key, another secret key is required. Thus, a circular problem is created that sounds almost like philosophers trying to define time in temporal terms! Fortunately, solutions are available (high-tech and very conventional!) for a secure secret key distribution!

On smaller networks where each participating NTP device is under the direct physical control of the network administrator, key distribution could actually be manual. The administrator knows what the key is, keeps it as a secret in his or her head, and physically goes from one device to another to perform the configuration. Additionally—even in the digital age where information can be transmitted almost instantaneously around the globe via the Internet—there is the possibility of distributing keys securely through such exotic means as courier services or registered mail. Unfortunately, the manual and/or courier approaches to key distribution break down extremely fast in larger, geographically dispersed network environments. Fortunately, several mechanisms have been developed and are available for private secret key distribution.

One of the mechanisms for private key distribution is the use of public key cryptography, which also happens to be part of the Autokey protocol. Public key cryptography is sometimes referred to as *asymmetric cryptography*. It relies on the use of two keys: public and private. If the public key is used to encrypt a message, then only the private key can be used to decrypt it, and vice versa. However, from the perspective of wanting to maintain secrecy between a sender and a receiver, it does not make much sense to be sending a message that's encrypted via one's private key.

When a sender encrypts a message using the recipient's public key, only the recipient can decrypt the message using his or her own private key. Imagine the opposite. The sender sends a message encrypting it via his or her own private key. Anybody with access to the recipient's public key (theoretically everybody!) could decrypt that message. That wouldn't exactly be a very secure system of communication, especially for the distribution of private keys for symmetric key cryptography! Sounds more like advertising!

The advantage of public key cryptography is obvious: a sender and a receiver can communicate securely without first having to exchange secret keys. The disadvantage is that public key cryptography is less efficient and more resource intensive than symmetric key cryptography. Also, public key cryptography does not lend itself to multicasting or broadcasting. When multiple recipients are involved in a communication process, a transmission from a sender to each recipient must be encrypted using each recipient's public key. Additionally, a mechanism must be in place to maintain the integrity of public keys, verify the identities of the public key owners, and provide authorized users with access to other users' public keys.

The expression *public* needs to be properly understood in the context of public key cryptography. Public keys are not lying around to be publicly viewed by everyone! Public keys are public in the sense that they can be made available to other users of public key cryptography services. In the commercial environments, public keys are maintained by companies that are referred to as *certification authorities* (CAs). Several companies (VeriSign, Thawte, GlobalSign, GeoTrust) offer numerous security services that include the issuance of certificates that can be used to distribute public keys to authorized users. Think of the commercial public key cryptography as a subscription service. Authorized subscribers can gain access to the public keys of other subscribers for the purpose of secure communication with them.

To learn about the cost of certificates, procedures for their procurement, how to install them on your system, and how they operate, the reader is encouraged to explore the websites of companies that offer certificate services. Public key cryptography services are also available through other means. For example, the OpenSSL library that's available for free supports public key cryptography. The OpenSSL software is recommended for use with the free distribution of NTP version 4. The OpenSSL library is available from http://www.openssl.org, and the most current release of NTP version 4 source files is available from http://www.ntp.org.

■**Note** It is the responsibility of every individual who downloads OpenSSL software to ensure compliance with governmental import/export regulations related to cryptography.

If an off-the-shelf software package or an operating system that is already in use on the network supports public key cryptography—including the generation of keys and the issuance of certificates—there might be no need to purchase a certificate from a commercial service for the purpose of key distribution. Or, as in the case of the free OpenSSL library and NTP version 4, the utility ntp-genkeys generates both public and private keys. Note, however, that the free NTP version 4 is in the form of source code. This means that NTP programs must first be compiled and successfully installed under a compatible operating system prior to any production-type NTP deployment and configuration. The operating systems for which the free NTP version 4 source code is available include Unix, Windows, and Virtual Memory System (VMS).

While the security considerations of each NTP deployment ought to be driven by a security policy and they cannot be easily reduced to a single hard and fast rule, it is a very reasonable approach for NTP administrators to consider public key cryptography for the purpose of key distribution while utilizing the symmetric key cryptography (it is more efficient!) for the purpose of actual authentication. The preceding recommendation is especially applicable to NTP version 3.

The Autokey Protocol

The Autokey protocol is fully described in an RFC memo (no number has been assigned to it yet!) that was published by David Mills under the title of "The Autokey Security Architecture, Protocols, and Algorithms" in August 2003. The Autokey protocol incorporates a number of security mechanisms to counter potential attempts to tamper with accurate and synchronized network timekeeping. The Autokey reference implementations are based on the Public Key Infrastructure (PKI) algorithms from within the OpenSSL library, which supports a range of message digests, digital signatures, and encryption methods. Other libraries that contain cryptographic functionality comparable to that of OpenSSL could be used for implementing Autokey as well.

The Autokey protocol combines several techniques to facilitate an efficient authentication of NTP sessions. Initially, Autokey relies on the PKI to generate a timestamped digital signature to sign a session key. However, if all of the subsequent packets between clients and servers carried a PKI signature, the computational load on the devices would simply be too great to be practical for any real-life NTP deployments. Consequently, to sustain the authentication process for subsequent sessions, Autokey has been designed to use a less computationally intensive algorithm of self-generated pseudo-random sequences of session keys (autokeys) and key IDs that together form an autokey list.

The Autokey protocol has three variations (also called *dances!*) that correspond to the different NTP operational modes: server/client, symmetric active/passive, and broadcast. See "NTP Modes of Operation and Associations" earlier in this chapter for more information about NTP modes. The Autokey operations vary somewhat between the dances, but generically the protocol performs the following functions in the course of facilitating secure authentication:

- **Detection of packet modifications via keyed message digests**: Functionally, this process is the same as with private key cryptography in NTPv3. The difference is that Autokey is based on public key cryptography and is available only in NTPv4.

- **Source identity verification via digital signatures**: This feature is unique to the Autokey protocol and is not available in NPTv3.

- **Cookie encryption**: In the context of NTP, cookies are 32-bit values that are used as one of the four components from which autokey values are computed. The other autokey components include the source and destination IP addresses and the key ID.

From the NTP configuration and troubleshooting perspective, the relevant Autokey characteristics include the following:

Backward compatibility: Autokey is backward compatible with NTPv3 symmetric key cryptography, which allows for the coexistence of NTPv3 and NTPv4 implementations in the same deployments. The compatibility is facilitated by dividing the key ID space in NTPv4 into two subspaces. The values of the symmetric key IDs are less than 65,536, while the pseudo-random values of the Autokey key IDs are equal to or greater than 65,536.

Key ID and key lifetime duration: The lifetimes of symmetric key IDs (and keys) are indefinite, while the Autokey key ID and key lifetimes are short, ranging in duration from that of a single polling interval (in practice 64 seconds or higher—see outputs in the "Sample Analysis of NTP Variables" section earlier in this chapter) to a maximum of about an hour. If the polling interval should be greater than one hour, a new key list is regenerated.

NTP packet modification: The NTP packet has been modified to accommodate the Autokey protocol. One or more extension fields have been added to the packet between the original header (ending with the transmit timestamp—see the "NTP Data Messages" section in Chapter 3 for more details on the NTP packet structure) and the optional authenticator. The optional authenticator field now contains the 128-bit message digest hash and the key ID, which collectively are referred to as the Massage Authentication Code (MAC).

Separate authentication for each NTP association: The Autokey protocol maintains a separate list of autokey sequences for each association, which in principle is similar to the operations of symmetric key cryptography where each association is independently authenticated.

While NTPv4 and the Autokey protocols have not yet been formally standardized, they are gradually making inroads into the NTP community and are bound to be showing up in upcoming NTP vendor implementations. See Chapter 5 for more information on the Autokey protocol configuration.

NTP Time Sources

Every NTP deployment must decide what the source of its reference time will be. The possible sources include

Dedicated NTP servers with access to an external UTC time source: These types of servers normally operate on private networks where it is deemed necessary by the network operating entity to have direct control over the location and configuration of the timeserver. An example of a dedicated NTP timeserver might be a Symmetricom's NTS-200 Stratum 1 server, which derives its UTC time from GPS satellites.

Public servers with or without direct access to UTC time: The "public" designation does not imply the server operational characteristics but rather its availability to the public. A server such as mentioned in the previous paragraph could be a public server if that server's network operating entity chose to make it so. Public servers are available over the Internet and, for practical purposes, vary in stratum levels from 1 to 3. The numbers of stratum 1 and 2 servers are in the hundreds; the number of public stratum 3 servers is in the thousands.

Local "masters" on the deployment network: These are devices that are configured with a time that's set by a network administrator. All other NTP devices synchronize their time with the master clock source time.

The choice of the time source for any NTP deployment should fall out from the design process. Administrators need to be mindful that not all public NTP servers offer accurate UTC time. Check out several public servers before deciding to synchronize your network's time to one of them! Also, the security of the public servers and the reliability of the transmission path between them and a synchronizing server on private networks are outside of the private networks administrators' control. With the master clock sources, the time may reset to some default bogus value when the master clock source device is powered down. The choice of the time source is part of the NTP design process, which is expanded upon in more detail in the next chapter.

Additional NTP Terms and Definitions

The terms and definitions that follow are intended as an additional reference to facilitate a better understanding of concepts that are expressed in this and other chapters. They do not represent a complete NTP glossary.

Clock accuracy: A measure of how well a clock's frequency and time compare with national standards.

Clock precision: A measure of how well (how precisely) the attributes of clock accuracy and stability can be maintained with a given timekeeping system.

Clock stability: A measure of how well a clock can maintain a constant frequency.

Drift: Mathematically, the second derivative of offset with respect to time. The first derivative of offset with respect to time.

Falseticker: An opposite of truechimer. The expression is used in reference to a clock that does not maintain timekeeping accuracy to a previously published trusted standard. An NTP configuration that uses public servers available over the Internet should take into account protection against falsetickers by specifying multiple public servers as outlined in Chapter 5.

Finite state machine: A state machine that's characterized by a specific or a finite number of possible states. For a complex state machine, such as a general-purpose computer itself with an operating system supporting numerous complex applications, the set of states is naturally finite but may be so large that some states may not even be known or defined at the time of the device release. In those cases, the more practical reference to a finite state machine is simply a state machine.

NTP association: An instantiation of a protocol machine. An association is normally formed when NTP peers (as per RFC 1305's definition of peers) exchange messages.

Offset: When it is used in reference to two clocks, offset represents the time difference between them.

Primary timeserver: An NTP device that incorporates a primary reference source (often referred to as a *reference clock*), which in turn is synchronized to national or international UTC time standards. Typically, a stratum 1 server would be considered as a primary timeserver. However, if a networking device is configured as a stratum 1 NTP server but it relies on its own local clock as a reference clock, that device would not be considered a primary timeserver. Instead, such a device could be labeled a local "master" time source or, as some vendors would have it, a "local-clock impersonator." That's quite a gap in labeling the same thing, from "master" to "impersonator"!

Private, dedicated NTP servers that incorporate a primary reference source, such as those discussed in the section "Choosing Your Time Source" in Chapter 5, qualify as primary timeservers. Most of the public stratum 1 servers available over the Internet should also qualify as primary timeservers, but there is no guarantee. As a function of your operating environment, you should be able to execute the `ntptrace` command (or equivalent) to determine what your primary timeserver is and what its primary reference source is.

Protocol machine: A special case of a finite state machine, specifically with regard to the operations of a particular protocol.

Reference clock: This expression is most frequently used to describe a radio or a GPS timecode receiver that is synchronized to a source of UTC time and that is also integrated into a primary timeserver via a reference clock driver. A reference clock is synonymous with a primary reference source in such cases (see "Primary time-server"). However, there is a special instance of a reference clock that's referred to as a pseudo-clock, when a device uses its local clock as a reference. A device may use a pseudo-clock when it becomes isolated from its primary time source or, in the case of higher stratum devices, from the primary timeservers.

Reference clock IP addressing: Reference clocks are identified via IP addresses in the format 127.127.t.u, where t specifies the clock type and u denotes the clock unit number. The values for t range from 1 up to the available number of reference clock drivers (40+ as of the time of writing). The values for u range from 0 to 3. There is an inherent assumption in this convention of no more than four clocks (0–3) of the same type within a single NTP device. And given that t could assume a value of up to 255, there is still plenty of room left for more different types of reference clocks to be developed. When the t value is 1, it represents the local clock—i.e., the pseudo-clock, the "master," the "impersonator," or whatever other labels the future may bring with regard to the local clock. The value of 127 in the first octet of the reference clock addresses indicates a reserved class A address. Internal loopback addresses also begin with 127. Any address that begins with 127 is a nonroutable address across network media and is valid only internally within a device.

Skew: A measure in hertz (cycles per second) of the difference between the actual frequency of a clock and what the clock frequency should be to maintain perfect time. When used in reference to two different clocks, skew is defined as the first derivative of the offset or the time difference between them.

State machine: In general, any device (mechanical or an abstraction as represented through software operations) that is able to maintain the status (the state) of an activity as a function of time. A state machine is able to respond to inputs to change a given status or state and is able to produce an output or take action in response to a change in state. Theoretically, every computer can be viewed as a state machine or, in actuality, a set of state machines with each application program and the operating system being a state machine. The concept of a state machine could be further applied to major components of an operating system, such as different protocol implementations, for example, thus allowing an operating system itself to be viewed as a set of state machines. In practice, a state machine that incorporates a set of functions supporting the operations of a particular protocol becomes a protocol machine.

Stratum: Numerical representation of the logical distance (the number of hops or intervening servers) that an NTP server is away from an external UTC clock source, which is typically in the form of a NIST radio station, GPS satellite, or CDMA cellular tower. A stratum 1 server has direct access to an external UTC clock source. The higher the stratum number, the further (logically) is the NTP server from the UTC source. The general formula is that an N stratum server is $N-1$ hops away from a UTC source. However, this formula is only a guideline that is subject to configuration best practices. It can be violated through improper NTP configuration.

Stratum 0 server: This expression is often used to identify a reference clock that's integrated into a primary timeserver, which in turn then becomes a stratum 1 server.

Time consumers: An expression that has been adopted by some vendors in reference to NTP devices (servers or clients) that are willing to have their time synchronized. This expression is typically used in conjunction with its corollary of *time providers*, which offer synchronization services to other NTP devices. As a function of configuration, NTP servers can assume the role of both, time consumers and time providers.

Time providers: An expression that has been adopted by some vendors in reference to servers that offer a synchronization service. This expression is typically used in conjunction with its corollary of time consumers.

Truechimer: A clock that maintains timekeeping accuracy to a previously published trusted standard.

NTP Design, Configuration, and Troubleshooting

Specific NTP configurations and deployment scenarios vary greatly as a function of the vast spectrum of network types and sizes that comprise the global networking environment. The specificity of each NTP configuration is further accentuated by the network equipment categories, end-user computing devices, operating systems, and equipment/OS vendors. However, as varied as the NTP deployment scenarios may be, the fundamental goal behind them remains the same: accurate and synchronized timekeeping among the participating devices.

Motivation for NTP Deployment on a Network

As with any networking protocol, the motivation for deployment and the approach to NTP configurations will vary widely, especially given the complex time-related relationships that permeate network use and administration. The section "Why the Need for NTP?" in Chapter 3 addresses the issue of motivation for NTP deployment in more detail with specific examples. To summarize, however, the motives regarding NTP deployment and types of resultant configurations are likely to be a combination and/or a variation of the following:

- **Need for transactional integrity:** With the growing popularity of automated business-to-business (B2B) and business-to-customer (B2C) electronic transactions as well as communications between individuals within and among businesses (collectively, *e-commerce*), the integrity of the transactions often hinges on the communicating parties being synchronized in time. Lack of transactional synchronization (even, if not absolute, time accuracy!) may have financial and legal implications due to disruptions in business logistics and operations.

- **Opportunity to perform future forensics**: Civil and criminal investigation, internal audits, and security breaches all may require suitable time-related evidence from across a spectrum of network devices that can be meaningful only if the devices are synchronized to an accurate time source.

- **Effective network administration**: Time-related network login procedures, backups, and routing stability all may be disrupted and invalidated as a result of inaccurate and not synchronized network time.

With so much at stake when it comes to accurate and synchronized network time, it behooves every network administrator to address the issue of NTP deployment and configuration with the attention that the process deserves. Improper NTP configuration may not cause loss of connectivity that results from malfunctioning Domain Name Service (DNS) configuration, for example, but the effects of NTP misconfiguration could be far subtler and less visible in real time, with far-reaching, long-range implications.

Approach to NTP Design and Configuration

Designing an effective NTP deployment is a process that embodies four key steps: choosing your time source, deciding upon the NTP topology, determining the NTP features to configure, and monitoring and managing NTP operations. Each step offers several choices that ultimately are a function of the network users' demand for accurate and synchronized network time. The careful consideration of the pros and cons of all the options that are outlined in the following four steps should lead to a successful NTP deployment regardless of the target network size, the topology, or even the available budget for ongoing network administration. For the purpose of NTP deployment, success is defined as a match between time accuracy expectations and the actual results. The four NTP deployment steps are as follows:

1. **Choose your NTP time source**: Given the wide range of NTP time source choices, this step sets the tone for the remainder of the design process, as it will impact the topology, configuration, and management aspects of NTP deployment. The NTP time source choices include

   - One or more private dedicated (as opposed to publicly available over the Internet) NTP stratum 1 timeservers with a reference clock that's synchronized to a primary source of UTC via GPS, CDMA, radio, or modem.

   - One or more public stratum 1 NTP servers available over the Internet. These are individual servers in contrast to the NTP timeserver pool.

- One or more public stratum 2 NTP servers available over the Internet. Similar to the stratum 1 public servers, these are individual servers in contrast to the NTP timeserver pool.

- NTP timeserver pool available over the Internet.

- A local "master" NTP device.

2. **Decide upon the NTP topology at the deployment site**: The NTP topology design will hinge upon the desired level for time accuracy with respect to UTC (microseconds, milliseconds, seconds, or hours) among the participating devices. The required level of time accuracy, in turn, is driven by the network use. The factors to consider in the NTP topology design stem from the requirement of an appropriate level of accuracy and include the following:

   - The number of NTP clients. This factor will determine the need for the presence of secondary, higher-stratum servers.

   - The existing level of network infrastructure redundancy. This factor will impact the level of redundancy in the NTP topology itself.

   - Network physical topology and geography. This factor will impact the type and consequently the quality of links between the NTP time source and clients. Varying round-trip delays impact NTP dispersion and affect time accuracy.

3. **Determine NTP features to configure**: A basic level of configuration is required for every networking protocol in order for it to function. Many other protocol features are optional but could be (and typically are!) extremely critical as a function of network use and requirements. In the case of NTP, the absolute minimum requirement is the identification of the NTP server on a client, provided that the server does not operate in a broadcast or multicast mode. Consider the following approach to NTP configuration, which begins with the required basics but is typically complemented with elements of some or all of the optional features and capabilities:

   - Basic features. Client/server identification. A more typical configuration would include elements of some or all of the optional features and capabilities that are listed next.

   - Security features. These include authentication and access control.

   - Redundant NTP time sources. The clients of lower-stratum servers that will act as servers to either higher-stratum servers or end-user clients could be configured with multiple time sources for the purpose of redundancy and increased potential for time accuracy.

- Operational modes. To increase scalability and ease NTP configuration, the broadcast, multicast, or manycast/anycast operational modes should be considered for both servers and clients. Always verify mode support for a given NTP implementation. SNTP and the evolving NTP version 4 offer the broadest operational mode support, which translates into configurations of unicast, broadcast, multicast, and manycast/anycast exchanges between clients and servers.

  - Additional configuration options. These options may include limiting the number of peers that can communicate with a given server, specifying the minimum poll interval (note that not all NTP implementations allow you to adjust the poll interval), and specifying the NTP source IP address (on routers the default source IP is the IP address of the interface through which the NTP packets are sent) plus any additional features that are bound to evolve as NTP matures as a function of time.

4. **Monitor and manage NTP operations**: The approach to NTP management will vary as a function of the NTP time source, the type of network management that's already implemented on the network, and the number of servers providing synchronization to the end clients.

Each of the preceding four steps is now considered in more detail.

Step 1: Choosing Your NTP Time Source

The choice of an NTP time source will be driven by factors that apply universally to all aspects of the network design process, not just NTP. Some of these factors include performance, reliability, the configuration interface, security, the ability to exercise direct control over the time source device, and, of course, the costs associated with securing or accessing a time source. One factor, however, that's entirely unique to the process of choosing the time source is the time source's accuracy.

Dedicated Private Timeserver

The following are clear advantages to using one or more private dedicated stratum 1 servers (primary timeservers) as your NTP time source:

Accuracy: These servers usually rely on GPS or the radio broadcast system to maintain their synchronization with UTC, typically to within a microsecond. GPS is ubiquitous, and each GPS satellite is equipped with several atomic clocks for redundancy. In the event that the link from a timeserver to a GPS satellite should fail, the timeserver configuration will determine how the timeserver can continue to operate. Temporarily, the timeserver could receive its time from an identical peer (a highly recommended topology option!), an optional oscillator that's installed within the timeserver, or other backup timeservers including those available over the Internet.

Security: You control the timeserver's physical placement location and access policy. And access to a dedicated timeserver is not likely to depend on your Internet connectivity, unless you are using the Internet to interconnect segments of your network via a Virtual Private Network (VPN). This means your NTP synchronization service is offered entirely on your internal network and behind a firewall, and the exchanges can also be easily encrypted, which is not necessarily an option when using public servers.

Availability: Given that these devices are single-purpose dedicated timeservers, they are not likely to be subject to application installations, operating system upgrades, configuration tweaking, or other tasks that in the course of the normal network administration would require the device to be either shut down or rebooted. Dedicated timeservers also tend to come with a very high Mean Time Between Failures (MBTF) value. A robust failover NTP design, with multiple units peering with each other and acting as backups, can further increase the inherent high availability of dedicated timeservers.

Ease of configuration and installation: Dedicated primary timeservers typically offer a web-based configuration capability, which simplifies the configuration process. In contrast, NTP configuration on Unix-based timeservers requires the creation of one or more config files (typically via a text editor) that are used by the xntpd/ntpd daemon. Creating config files in the Unix environment is generally considered to be more error-prone and requires a greater skill level than the use of a web-based configuration method. Additionally, if the xntpd/ntpd daemon already comes with a Unix-based software distribution, then at least you need not be concerned about compiling the latest distribution of NTP source code and making sure you have the right device drivers for any reference clocks to be supported by the daemon. Otherwise, there is extra time and effort that goes into setting up an NTP primary timeserver from the free NTP distribution. However, regardless of the type of primary timeserver you decide to use (dedicated or Unix based for which you compiled the xntpd/ntpd daemon), if it incorporates a GPS-based receiver, you will need to install an antenna and the appropriate cabling.

The preceding advantages of dedicated timeservers should translate in the network administrators' minds into a degree of comfort and relaxation with respect to NTP design and maintenance—not that IS managers want their net administrators to be comfortable or relaxed! However, it would be nice to have some network equipment operate so well and with no or absolutely minimal demand for attention that it would be altogether easy to forget about its existence. Additionally, dedicated NTP timeservers are capable of supporting thousands of clients, which could significantly simplify the overall NTP topology and client configuration by making the topology flat instead of hierarchical.

The obvious disadvantage of a dedicated private server might be its cost, especially in light of a large number of public servers being readily accessible over the Internet. However, the cost factor always needs to be considered in the context of all the advantages and disadvantages of the dedicated timeserver solution. Physically, a dedicated timeserver is typically a rack-mounted device (1 U) with an RJ-45 Ethernet interface to the network and a serial port. Figure 5-1 illustrates Symmetricom's high-performance GPS timeserver, model NTS-200.

Figure 5-1. *Symmetricom's model NTS-200 GPS network timeserver. Reprinted with permission from Symmetricom.*

Public Server(s) or NTP Pool

The decision of whether the cost of a dedicated NTP server is justifiable could hinge on the following considerations:

- The degree of a public (offsite) server's availability over the Internet

- The level of a public server's security, accuracy, and load

- The impact of a public server's use on your network security

The preceding considerations ultimately impact your ability to maintain accurate and synchronized time on your network.

Public Server's Availability Consideration

Consideration of a public server's availability should take into account the reliability of connections from the deployment site to the Internet, the physical location of the public server(s) on the Internet (typically, you should consider one that's located in your own country or at least on the same continent), and the routing path (number of hops) between the server(s) and the deployment site. Usually, the more hops between a timeserver and the deployment site, the bigger the potential for longer round-trip delays as well as network outages along the path.

Tip A simple ping to the candidate server(s) will give you an idea of the round-trip delays between your site and the server(s).

The round-trip delays between the NTP client on your network and the public servers impact the level of dispersion that is normally displayed in all NTP implementations when viewing NTP associations. As a network administrator, you have no control over the quality of service on the Internet. This means that poor service quality along the path from your NTP client to a public server could prevent you from using a public server. Again, the need for accuracy will be a deciding factor.

Note As a rule of thumb, if your desired accuracy is in microseconds, chances are that you will not be able to rely on public servers and you should be looking at purchasing a dedicated stratum 1 primary time-server. For accuracy requirements in milliseconds, the recommendation is to monitor the dispersion levels if you are using public servers. For accuracy requirements in seconds, you should be fine relying on public servers. That's unless you have the statistical misfortune to synchronize with multiple falsetickers beyond the ability of the NTP algorithms to detect that condition!

An additional issue to consider regarding public servers' availability is that they may become unavailable for extended periods of time or entirely go offline without notification for reasons including maintenance, a failure, or a decision to no longer provide time service. It's not uncommon for installations relying on public servers to have their client configurations point to nonexistent IP addresses or domain names of onetime operational public timeservers. On the surface, if redundancy is properly configured, having a public timeserver become unavailable for a period of time might not represent a major disruption to your time service. However, if network administration procedures are not in place for the detection of public timeservers going offline, over a period of time you may end up relying solely on local clocks or, worse, getting your time from a single false-ticker that could end up creating havoc with your record keeping. Industries where accurate timekeeping is especially critical (such as healthcare for administering drugs and maintaining patient records and emergency response for accurately reconstructing activities in life-threatening scenarios) should pay particular attention to the availability issue of the public timeservers.

Public Server's Security, Accuracy, and Load Consideration

The level of security, accuracy, and load on public servers is likely to be a function of their access policies, which are as follows:

Open access: Any client from any location can use the public server without obtaining prior permission from the server administrator. While this open policy is convenient for gaining access quickly to one or more public NTP servers, the policy does not necessarily bode well for a high degree of accuracy in mission-critical environments. Public server performance could be degraded by a large number of clients, as there is no obvious mechanism for controlling access.

Restricted access: The specifics of access restriction will vary from one server to another, but generally a restricted access policy implies geographical constraints, client stratum level constraints, or user type constraints. For example, a restricted access policy may be that the server provides open access to stratum 2 servers, but for all other types of connections (clients or higher-stratum servers) prior arrangements must be with the server administrator. Or the server could be available to educational institutions but not commercial enterprises. Additionally, restricted access could also be in place to limit the number of clients.

Closed access: An NTP public server with a closed access policy sounds like a contradiction in terms, but it generally means you must contact the server administrator prior to making any connections to use the server as your time source. In the listing of public servers with a closed access policy, the IP address of the server is going to be blanked out.

No precise formula correlates the server security, accuracy, and load to the server access policy. However, in general, consider that the more restricted the server access policy, the more likely that someone is concerned about that server's operations. Consequently, the server's security and accuracy are likely to be higher, while its load is likely to be more closely monitored and managed than for servers with a completely open access policy. It seems natural that in mission-critical environments (if you decide to rely on public servers to begin with!), you want to ensure the maximum security, accuracy, and availability of your NTP time source, which translates into a certain amount of footwork (contacting the server administrators and making arrangements for server use) to select the most reliable public NTP servers(s). Also, always be sure to follow the instructions on the server use, even if the server happens to be an open-policy server that requires no arrangements prior to its use.

■**Note** As a general rule, keep in mind that public servers are administered on a voluntary basis, regardless of their access policies. The resultant implication is lack of guarantees for server availability, accuracy, and security. But just because IP is a connectionless and "unreliable" protocol does not mean that one should not be using it. Until such time (if ever) that IP is replaced by another protocol, today's Internet would cease to exist without it!

When considering public server(s) as your time source, consider also the NTP pool server approach, where instead of using specific servers (identified by the unique IP addresses or DNS names) you define your NTP server configuration statements at the deployment site as pointing to a server pool. NTP server pools are identified by generic names such as 0.pool.ntp.org, 1.pool.ntp.org, 2.pool.ntp.org, and more that usually relate to the pool's geographical location. Those names point to groups of servers that participate in the NTP server pooling project. The servers within a group rotate on a periodic basis, which means there is a measure of natural load balancing that goes on, and no single public server participating in the pool is likely to become overloaded. At least, that's the initial theory and motivation behind NTP server pooling.

However, while the overall server availability may be enhanced through the concept of the pool, consider also that the quality of the time received from those servers may be less than ideal, given that the servers in the pool could come from all over the world and varied levels of administration expertise. Since NTP server pools for different continents are now also becoming available, those might be better candidates than the generic pools.

■**Tip** For more information about NTP pool servers, visit `http://www.pool.ntp.org`.

It is recommended that when considering using public server(s), the designer first verify the accuracy (at least as being reasonable) of the servers' time. While it may be generally assumed that a stratum 1 public server is going to be synchronized to an external reliable reference clock, that is not necessarily the case. Public stratum 1 servers could technically be using their own internal clocks. In fact, it's not a bad idea to assume the worst-case scenario that a public server you are considering for your time source is a falseticker.

■**Caution** To guard against falsetickers, consider using multiple public servers in your configuration. The emerging consensus among NTP geeks and heavyweights (based on algorithms outside the scope of this publication!) is that the use of one to three public servers in your configuration does not protect you against a falseticker among them. Four seems to be the number that offers protection against a single false-ticker lurking in their midst. Using more than four servers in your configuration might be acceptable from a technical point of view, but at a certain point common sense has to kick in. After all, you are relying on public resources—in all likelihood for a commercial purpose. While there may not be a formal Acceptable Use Policy (AUP) with regard to public NTP servers, it is always advisable to exercise reason and common sense when using them as your time sources, lest your desire for greater accuracy becomes a form of abuse.

The rule-of-thumb formula for using public servers to protect you against falsetickers is that the number of servers (time sources) should be $2n + 1$, where n is the number of possible falsetickers within the group. This statement immediately contradicts what was stated in the preceding note in the case of $n = 1$, which happens to be the exception to this rule of thumb. But as the saying goes, the exception confirms a rule!

When $n = 2$, using five servers should protect you against two falsetickers, and when $n = 3$, using seven public servers should offer protection against three falsetickers among them. With $n = 4$, you are looking at configuring nine servers. With nine servers, however, consider yourself on the threshold of abusive behavior! It follows from the preceding that using a single public server is not necessarily recommended unless its accuracy and reliability has been verified through external means and you are prepared to deal with the implications of a single point of failure with regard to your time source. It's back to design criteria: what level of time inaccuracy or lack of synchronization can your network tolerate?

The Impact of Public NTP Servers' Use on Your Network's Security

The impact of a public NTP server's use on your network's security complements the initial public server security consideration, which relates to the server's physical and administrative environment over which you have no control to begin with! If an NTP client on your network (assume a scenario with a stratum 2 server on your network acting as a client to a stratum 1 public server on the Internet) is behind a firewall, then the firewall will need to be configured to allow UDP traffic on port 123 to pass through it. Also, chances are that the NTP traffic between your NTP client/server and the public server will be transmitted in the clear (unencrypted), making the NTP packets subject to tampering by intruders.

Thus, the combination of allowing traffic on port 123 through a firewall, having NTP packets transmitted in the clear, and encountering the uncertainty over the administrative/security environment of the public servers themselves should give security-conscious network administrators pause to think about the collective implications of these factors on the security of their networks. Access control configuration based on the IP addresses of the servers can harden somewhat the security of deployments that rely on public servers, but it also lends itself to potential disruptions in the event that the IP addresses of the servers change while their DNS names remain the same. The key to successfully deploying public servers is to be fully aware of all the implications of their use: availability, accuracy, and security. And NTP security should always be considered in the context of the security policy for the entire network.

A Local NTP "Master" Device

When choosing an NTP time source, a designer might also consider the option of using and configuring an existing network device as a local NTP "master." A local NTP "master" relies on a local time source (time determined and set by you), which is not synchronized with UTC. The use of the "master" feature facilitates time synchronization among the participating devices based on the local time, even if that time is not highly accurate with relation to UTC. A local NTP "master" could be a router, a switch, or a server that implements the "master" feature.

■**Caution** Not all NTP implementations support the "master" feature.

Given that the primary purpose of a local NTP "master" is other than time synchronization, consider the use of the "master" feature as a no-cost option, similar from a budgetary perspective to the use of public NTP servers available over the Internet.

Summary of NTP Time Sources Features

Table 5-1 summarizes the key features (availability, accuracy, security, and cost) of the three categories of NTP time sources: dedicated server, public servers, and local "master." Each feature is rated based on one of three values: high, medium, or low. While the features are distinct from one another, there is also a close relationship between them. For example, low security could definitely impact a server's availability and compromise its accuracy. It's not surprising that a dedicated server is a clear winner from a technical point of view. But it also comes at a price. The decision to use one time source vs. another is ultimately a network design decision based on requirements and available budget.

Table 5-1. *Feature Summary of NTP Time Sources*

Time Source	Availability	Accuracy	Security	Cost
Dedicated server	High	High	High	High
Public server(s)	Medium	Medium	Low	Low
Local "master"	High	Low	High	Low

Step 2: Deciding Upon NTP Topology at Deployment Site

Following the selection of the NTP time source(s), the next major decision in the NTP design process is to determine the NTP topology at the deployment site. Any decision that involves topology will be driven by the size of the network, specifically the number of clients participating in the NTP exchanges, the need for redundancy in offering the NTP service, and the actual physical layout of the network.

The Number of NTP Clients

One of the challenges with NTP terminology is that the same physical NTP entities wear multiple hats as a function of their interactions with other NTP devices. When considering the number of clients at a deployment site, the word *client* is used to mean any NTP device at the site other than the primary time source(s), which were discussed in the preceding "Step 1: Choosing Your NTP Time Source" section. Those clients are bound to include one or more servers that will be synchronizing their time with the primary time sources, in all likelihood one or more of the Internet public servers or pool. In turn, those newly become clients/servers may also peer with one another (be configured at the same stratum level but at a higher one than the primary time source) to facilitate a degree of redundancy, thus giving them a third hat, that of a peer.

The simplest NTP topology involves a single NTP server synchronizing the clocks of all other NTP devices. In the case of a private dedicated NTP server that's capable of servicing thousands of clients, the use of a single server approach (without any intervening higher-stratum servers to create an NTP hierarchy) may work quite well even for larger networks. Some degree of traffic analysis may be appropriate to ensure that the NTP traffic between the server and all of the other clients will not disrupt regular network operations.

The rule-of-thumb formula regarding the relationship between NTP topology and the number of clients is to use point-to-point topology (unicast client/server exchanges) at the top of the NTP hierarchy while relying more on broadcast, multicast, and anycast/manycast (point-to-multipoint and multipoint-to-point) operations as the hierarchy progresses outward toward the end users. Although dedicated primary timeservers can support thousands of clients, allowing for the flattening of the NTP hierarchy (and topology!), with multipurpose NTP servers (devices such as routers, switches, and servers, whose primary function is not NTP synchronization) it's best to keep the number of clients to a single server at no more than a few hundred.

The Level of Network Redundancy

In the context of the TCP/IP stack, NTP is an application service that rides on top of the lower layers: hardware (physical and data link), network, and transport. Consequently, the level of redundancy within the network infrastructure itself (OSI layers 1 through 4) impacts the design of redundancy for application services, including NTP. For example, assume a hub-and-spoke network infrastructure design—a central office/headquarters with multiple branches, as illustrated in Figure 5-2—which is a common networking topology for many industries including finance, retail, and manufacturing.

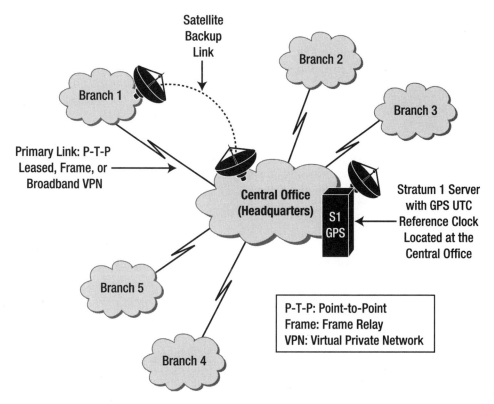

Figure 5-2. *Hub-and-spoke network infrastructure design*

If the design of the links between the branches and the central location is sufficiently robust, with a swift failover to backup links in the event of primary link failures, then the NTP application service (assume one of the time sources from the section "Step 1: Choosing Your NTP Time Source") could reside at the central location. The NTP service would be administered to all the clients at the branches from the central location either directly—without any additional higher-stratum servers—or indirectly, through higher-stratum servers at the branches. The NTP topology becomes very simple: a primary time source at the central location with clients that might include secondary timeservers, possibly as a function of the total number of clients at the branches. This NTP topology would be taking advantage of the robustness of the underlying networking infrastructure.

Suppose, however, that in Figure 5-2 the links between the branches and the central location are not very robust and no provisions exist for failover to backup links. Link outages are frequent. However, the design of the actual end-user computing applications at the branches is such that they are able to operate in both local and central modes (local when a link goes down and central when a link is up) for extended periods of time. In this scenario, relying on the NTP service to be delivered from the central location might be considered a poor design decision. The level of NTP redundancy should be brought in line with the redundancy design for all the other applications, i.e., the ability to function effectively without access to the central office.

Whatever the NTP time source happens to be at the central location (dedicated server, public servers, or local "master"), the less robust infrastructure would seem to point in the direction of having a secondary timeserver at each branch that synchronizes its time with multiple sources: a primary timeserver at the central office and in all likelihood several public servers available over the Internet. Should security considerations preclude the use of public servers, the choice becomes clear if a premium is placed on time synchronization and accuracy: make the infrastructure more robust, or place a dedicated private server at each branch. Alternatively, have a local "master" administer time for each branch. The last alternative is hardly recommended if a high degree of accuracy and synchronization is required throughout the entire enterprise.

Impact of Network Physical Topology and Geography on NTP Topology

Physical network topology and geography are closely related to the quality and reliability of the network infrastructure, especially where a large number of WAN links may be involved in an internetwork. For example, the lack of robust WAN services in a given geographical area can, out of necessity, lead to the provisioning of lower bandwidth and less reliable links. When low bandwidth is coupled with the bursty nature of network traffic between various locations, the two factors can significantly impact the level of link utilization, thus leading to congestion at certain peak times. Network congestion, in turn, will impact round-trip delays between NTP servers and clients, ultimately impacting the time accuracy. If enhancing the quality of infrastructure is out of the question because of geographical or other constraints, then the NTP topology should reflect that fact and be more distributed than hierarchical: each geographical area and/or major network section ought to plan on having its own time source.

Step 3: Determining NTP Features to Configure

Determining what NTP features to configure represents the third and last major step in the generic approach to NTP design and configuration. While it is still possible to find earlier implementations of NTP (versions 1 and 2), the configuration examples that follow pertain to NTPv3, the evolving NTPv4, and SNTP. The examples relate to the basic NTP configuration (configuration statements that enable the NTP process and allow it to function at the most basic level), NTP security, NTP redundancy, NTP operational modes, and other options.

■Note In the context of NTP configuration, many of the networking vendors have adopted the use of the expression *NTP peer* in reference to NTP devices that offer synchronization service and are also willing to be synchronized, i.e., devices that operate at the same functional level. Thus, peers could be groups of two or more stratum 1 or stratum 2 servers that synchronize with one another. From the perspective of NTP modes, the concept of NTP peers translates into two or more NTP devices operating in a symmetric active mode (mode type 1). The exact syntax of the NTP peer configuration may vary under different operating systems. In general, however, when two or more devices are each configured with one or more "peer" statements (with the "peer" statement followed by an IP address of one of the other devices in the group), they are considered to be in a peer as opposed to a client/server relationship. Note that the industry use of *peer* varies from the terminology of RFC 1305 (as explained in the section "NTP Servers, Clients, Hosts, and Peers" in Chapter 4). But the industry use of the *peer* expression makes intuitive sense, especially in the context of NTP configuration.

Basic NTP Configuration

Basic NTP configuration will vary depending on what's being configured: server, client, or peer. There will also be variation as a function of the operating system. But in general, the basic configuration allows a client to receive updates from a server, a server to offer updates, and peers to exchange updates. Basic NTP configuration would not address NTP security or redundancy.

Basic Dedicated Timeserver Configuration

Figure 5-3 and Figure 5-4 illustrate the basic configuration of a dedicated timeserver via a web-based interface for Symmetricom's SyncServer S100 model. While the configuration screen offers many options within several categories, the basic configuration involves selecting the role in which this device will operate (server, peer, etc.), as shown in Figure 5-3, and then configuring the IP addressing and DNS, as shown in Figure 5-4.

   Note the minimum and maximum polling interval options in Figure 5-3. NTP devices that use a command-line interface (CLI) or a configuration file normally specify the parameters for these options as an exponent of the power of 2. Thus, a minimum interval of 1 minute and 4 seconds (64 seconds) translates into a minimum poll interval value of 6 (2 * 6 = 64), while the maximum poll of 17 minutes and 4 seconds (1,024 seconds) translates into a maximum poll interval value of 10 (2 * 10 = 1024). Listing 5-2 demonstrates a minimum and maximum poll interval values configuration from the CLI.

■Note For more information about Symmetricom's timeservers, visit http://www.ntp-systems.com.

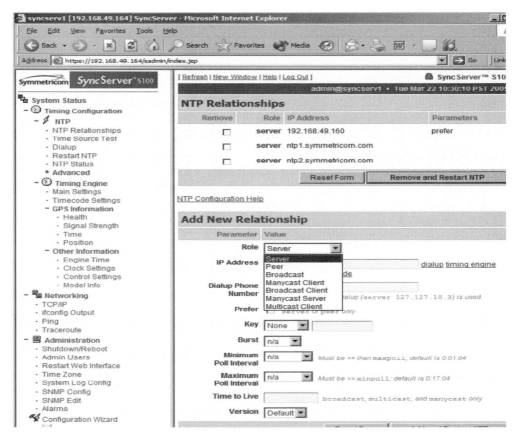

Figure 5-3. *Device role configuration screen for Symmetricom's SyncServer S100 dedicated timeserver*

Basic Unix/Linux NTP Client Configuration

In the Unix/Linux environments, the NTP configuration is stored in the xntp.conf (version 3) or ntp.conf (version 4) file that resides in the /etc directory. The xntpd/ntpd daemon, which represents the complete implementation of version 3 or version 4.*x* of NTP, reads the commands from the configuration file at startup time. Some xntpd/ntpd implementations allow you to override the configuration file name from the command line, but the stated names represent the default, commonly used ones. The Unix/Linux NTP implementations that are referenced here pertain to Sun's Solaris, IBM's AIX, SCO's OpenServer Release, HP's HP-UX, Red Hat's Linux, and other Unix-flavor operating systems. The reader is always encouraged to consult each product's manual for the most up-to-date and specific syntax of xntpd/ntpd-related commands and their associated parameters. In general, however, the statements in a basic xntp.conf or ntp.conf configuration file will include those illustrated in Listing 5-1.

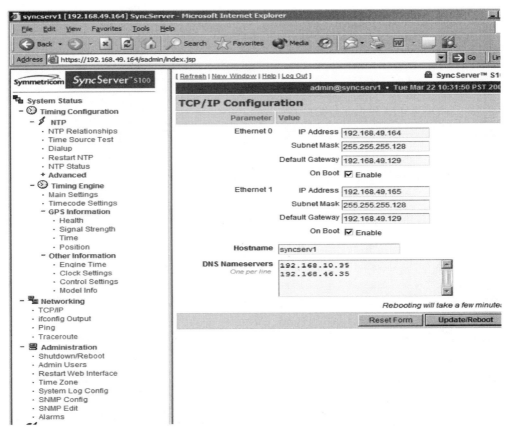

Figure 5-4. *TCP/IP configuration screen for Symmetricom's SyncServer S100 dedicated timeserver*

Listing 5-1. *Contents of a Basic* npt.conf *Configuration File*

```
server  xxx.xxx.xxx.xxx
server  127.127.1.0
fudge   127.127.1.0 stratum 10
driftfile /var/lib/ntp/ntp.drift
```

The xxx.xxx.xxx.xxx in Listing 5-1 represents the IP address of a device acting as an NTP server to this client. The 127.127.1.0 address represents the local clock (also referred to as *undisciplined* local clock), which is intended to act as a backup in case the connectivity to the xxx.xxx.xxx.xxx server is lost. The fudge command that normally follows the server command that's referencing the local clock can be used with several optional parameters. In the preceding example, the fudge command uses only the stratum option to identify a high stratum level. A high stratum number is assigned to the local clock (a stratum value that's higher than any operational value within the network) so in the event that connectivity is lost to the xxx.xxx.xxx.xxx server—and the undisciplined backup local clock becomes the reference clock—other clients that might be pointing to this device will not attempt to synchronize their time to it.

■**Note** Listing 5-1 represents a special case use of the `fudge` command on client devices. On a primary timeserver, the `fudge` command is normally used with a `time1` parameter, and the IP address that's used with the command points to the reference clock that's integrated into the primary timeserver.

The `driftfile` command identifies the location of the drift file. The purpose of the drift file is to record the drift, which is also referred to as the *frequency error,* or the frequency offset of the local clock oscillator. Since we live in an imperfect world, the clocks within computing devices tend not to operate at absolutely constant frequencies, in part even as a result of temperature variations. NTP algorithms can take the frequency offset into account in order to maintain greater clock accuracy.

The initial frequency offset is assumed to be zero if the `driftfile` command is not specified in the configuration or the drift file does not yet exist. The `xntpd/ntpd` daemon maintains the drift file and needs to have write permission in the directory where the file is located. If the drift file does not exist when the `xntpd/ntpd` daemon is started, the daemon creates the file after about an hour of operation with the value of the frequency offset in it. If the drift file exists when the `xntpd/ntpd` daemon is started, the daemon uses the value of the offset stored in the file for its calculations and updates that value accordingly.

Basic Unix/Linux NTP Primary Timeserver Configuration

The basic NTP primary timeserver configuration in a Unix/Linux environment is similar in context to that of the NTP client configuration. The big operational difference is that the IP address following the `server` command is in the form 127.127.t.u, which means that the IP address points to a reference clock that must be supported by the `xntpd/ntpd` daemon via an appropriate driver. A reference clock is typically a radio or a GPS receiver that's physically integrated into the timeserver (to make it a primary timeserver) via a serial interface. See Chapter 4's "Additional NTP Terms and Definitions" section for an explanation of the 127.127.t.u IP address format.

Listing 5-2 illustrates a configuration that would be applicable to an HP-UX machine with an HP58503A GPS receiver to turn it into a primary timeserver.

Listing 5-2. *Basic NTP Configuration on a Primary Timeserver*

```
server  127.127.26.1 minpoll minpoll_value maxpoll maxpoll_value
fudge 127.127.26.1 time1 time1_value
```

In Listing 5-2, the t (type) value of the 127.127.26.1 IP address is 26, which represents the Hewlett-Packard 58503A GPS Receiver (HP_GPS). The minpoll and maxpoll parameters represent minimum and maximum polling intervals for reference clock messages in seconds to the power of 2. For example, if minpoll=3 and maxpoll=4, the minimum polling interval would be 8 seconds, and the maximum polling interval would be 16 seconds.

The fudge command, in contrast to the client configuration where it was used with the stratum parameter, is used with the time1 parameter. Time1 specifies a constant that's to be added to the time offset and used as a calibration constant. The value of time1 should be supplied by the GPS/radio receiver vendor and may vary even for the same receiver as a function of the platform (PC type) with which it is installed.

In scenarios that use multiple primary Unix/Linux timeservers, the basic configuration shown in Listing 5-2 would be (or perhaps should be!) complemented with peer statements for the purpose of creating NTP redundancy between the servers.

Typical Unix/Linux Client Configuration

The ntp.conf file as shown in Listing 5-3 illustrates a more typical configuration that's found on Unix clients. This configuration implements redundancy and an access policy, which is intended to reduce the chance of an attacker (or an inexperienced administrator!) being able to exploit any vulnerabilities of the ntpd daemon.

Listing 5-3. *Typical* ntp.conf *File*

```
#  Define the default access policy
restrict default ignore

# Synchronize with three timeservers for redundancy
server XXX.XXX.XXX.XXX
server YYY.YYY.YYY.YYY
server ZZZ.ZZZ.ZZZ.ZZZ

#Restrict run-time modifications, peering, queries,
#and trap service from the three timeservers
restrict XXX.XXX.XXX.XXX nomodify nopeer noquery notrap
restrict YYY.YYY.YYY.YYY nomodify nopeer noquery notrap
restrict ZZZ.ZZZ.ZZZ.ZZZ nomodify nopeer noquery notrap
```

```
# Use the local clock (the impersonator or the local "master")
#if the timeservers become unavailable
server  127.127.1.0
fudge   127.127.1.0 stratum 10

#Restrict run-time modifications, peering, queries,
#and trap service from IPs beginning with 127
# i.e., all possible reference clocks
restrict 127.0.0.0 mask 255.0.0.0 nomodify nopeer noquery notrap

#Define the location for a drift file. Make sure the location permits write access
driftfile /etc/ntp.drift
```

The restrict command facilitates access control to this host. Even though this host synchronizes with multiple servers (identified via the XXX.XXX.XXX.XXX, YYY.YYY.YYY.YYY, ZZZ.ZZZ.ZZZ.ZZZ IP addresses), it also restricts those servers with respect to the NTP services and/or operations they can perform on and/or with it. The functions of the parameters that are used with the restrict command (nomodify, nopeer, noquery, notrap) relate to the actions of the NTP control messages, which are identified via the mode value of 6 or 7 in the NTP message header.

See Chapter 3's "NTP Data Messages" and "NTP Control Messages" sections for the meaning of the mode variable and possible actions resulting from the use of control messages, as specified by the operation code in the NTP control message header. The meaning of the specific parameters that are used with the restrict command in Listing 5-3 is as follows:

Nomodify: Ignore all of the NTP control packets that attempt to modify the state of the timeserver; i.e., alter the run-time configuration. However, if this is the only parameter that's used with the restrict command, any of the three timeservers in Listing 5-3 could still establish a peering relationship (active symmetric mode), perform queries, and receive time service from this host. Additional parameters are thus used to further limit the interactions of the timeserver(s) with this host.

Nopeer: Provide a stateless time service to the polling devices, but do not permit the establishment of a peering relationship with them. This parameter prevents this host from being in a symmetric active mode with the timeserver that's identified in the restrict command.

Noquery: Ignore all NTP control packets that represent queries and/or configuration requests from the timeserver. These packets are generated via the ntpq and/or ntpdc utilities.

Notrap: Ignore all NTP control messages that solicit trap service to the timeserver. The values of 6 and 7 in the control message operation code field (not to be confused with the values of 6 and 7 in the mode field!) relate to SNMP trap operations.

Additional parameters are available for use with the `restrict` command. Given the "private use" designation of the mode value of 7 in the NTP message header—to signify a class of private NTP control messages—there is a potential for ongoing development of new command parameters as well as the creation of new NTP-related utilities that will rely on that mode value. The reader is always referred to each vendor's documentation for their particular release of NTP for the exact list of available NTP commands and corresponding parameters. The following are the few additional parameters that are commonly used with the `restrict` command:

Ignore: This parameter instructs the host to ignore all NTP packets from devices that match this entry. In Listing 5-3 this parameter is used without an IP address/mask combination and in conjunction with the `default` parameter, which signifies the definition of a default access policy that is then subject to modification by other `restrict` commands. When the `restrict` command is used without an IP address/mask, it means it matches all incoming packets. Thus, a common approach to setting up an NTP access policy is to deny access to all incoming NTP packets by default. Subsequent `restrict` commands then modify the default policy. This is not unlike denying all traffic to an internal network through a firewall and then selectively allowing traffic based on the security policy for that network.

Noserve: This parameter permits NTP control packets (mode value of 6 or 7) but ignores other packets, effectively denying time services to the devices as identified by the IP addresses in the `restrict` command. This parameter is not used in Listing 5-3. However, it could be used to complement the other parameters on timeservers identified via the XXX.XXX.XXX.XXX, YYY.YYY.YYY.YYY, and ZZZ.ZZZ.ZZZ.ZZZ addresses, or it could be used with another host IP address (or network) to deny devices that match those addresses from accessing NTP synchronization from this host.

Default: This is technically not a parameter but rather a keyword that's used with the `restrict` command to signify the default IP address/mask combination of 0.0.0.0/0.0.0.0 that matches all incoming entries. When other parameters are used with the `default` keyword, an initial (default!) access policy is set up that is then subject to modification by subsequent `restrict` command statements.

Additional parameters above and beyond those listed are available for use with the `restrict` command, and the reader is referred to each vendor's documentation for their exact syntax and meaning. In all likelihood, even more parameters will become available as NTP continues to evolve.

Basic Cisco Router/Switch NTP Configuration

Cisco routers and switches are typically deployed as secondary timeservers, which means that even as they serve time to other devices and peer with them as well, those among them with the lowest stratum number will be using a dedicated private timeserver, a public timeserver, or a local "master" as their time source.

The basic client configuration with no NTP security features on a Cisco device is thus reduced to determining the time source, the operational mode, and what IP addresses to use for forming NTP associations. Listing 5-4 illustrates a basic Cisco router NTP configuration. Subsequent examples illustrate similar configurations but on a Cisco switch that offers a different configuration interface.

Listing 5-4. *Basic Cisco Router (Client Mode) NTP Configuration*

```
Router1#configure terminal
Enter configuration commands, one per line.  End with CNTL/Z.
Router1(config)#ntp server 172.16.21.1
Router1(config)#ntp source serial0
Router1(config)#
```

The configuration in Listing 5-4 identifies the NTP server and the interface whose IP address will be used to form associations. A common approach is to define a loopback interface and use its IP for forming NTP associations, since loopback interfaces are less prone to flapping than physical ones. The private IP address in the server command implies that it's not a public server, as private addresses are not routable over the Internet. This means the timeserver for this client is either a dedicated private server or, more likely, another Cisco device that has been defined as a local "master" via an ntp master command. Since there are no peer statements in this configuration, the operational mode should end up being that of the client (mode value of 3) as confirmed by a detailed display resulting from the show ntp associations detail command in Listing 5-5.

Listing 5-5. *Output from* show ntp associations detail *Command for a Cisco Router with the Basic Client Mode Configuration from Listing 5-4*

```
Router1#show ntp associations detail
172.16.21.1 configured, our_master, sane, valid, stratum 8
ref ID 127.127.7.1, time C6B20863.17B557A2 (19:52:03.092 UTC Sat Aug 20 2005)
our mode client, peer mode server, our poll intvl 64, peer poll intvl 64
root delay 0.00 msec, root disp 0.03, reach 377, sync dist 6.042
delay 8.50 msec, offset -8.6081 msec, dispersion 1.77
precision 2**19, version 3
org time C6B20875.B0D1F24E (19:52:21.690 UTC Sat Aug 20 2005)
rcv time C6B20875.B4C52984 (19:52:21.706 UTC Sat Aug 20 2005)
xmt time C6B20875.B1E70769 (19:52:21.694 UTC Sat Aug 20 2005)
filtdelay =    11.05    8.50    8.77    8.77    8.41    8.47    8.44    8.38
filtoffset =   -9.90   -8.61   -8.48   -8.41   -8.07   -7.91   -7.74   -7.36
filterror =     0.02    0.99    1.97    2.94    3.92    4.90    5.87    6.85
```

■Note The use of the word *peer* in the preceding display is in accordance with the definition of the term in RFC 1305.

The subsequent examples, Listing 5-6 and Listing 5-7, show two options for the basic client configuration on Cisco 6500 series Catalyst switches. The first option is to enable the client (switch) to receive NTP broadcast updates from an NTP broadcast server. The second option is to identify the server by its IP address.

Listing 5-6. *Cisco Client Switch Configured to Receive NTP Broadcasts from a Server*

```
Console> (enable) set ntp broadcastclient enable
NTP Broadcast Client mode enabled
Console> (enable) set ntp broadcastdelay 5000
NTP Broadcast delay set to 5000 microseconds
Console> (enable) show ntp
Current time: Sat Aug 20 2005, 21:53:31
Timezone: '', offset from UTC is 0 hours
Summertime: '', disabled
Last NTP update:
Broadcast client mode: enabled
Broadcast delay: 5000 microseconds
Client mode: disabled
NTP-Server
-----------------------------------------
Console> (enable)
```

Listing 5-7. *Cisco Client Switch Configured with an IP Address of a Server*

```
Console> (enable) set ntp server 172.25.12.6
NTP server 172.25.12.6 added.
Console> (enable) set ntp client enable
NTP Client mode enabled
Console> (enable) show ntp
Current time: Sat Aug 20 2005, 22:01:14
Timezone: '', offset from UTC is 0 hours
Summertime: '', disabled
Last NTP update: Sat Aug 20 2005, 22:01:01
Broadcast client mode: disabled
Broadcast delay: 3000 microseconds
Client mode: enabled
NTP-Server
-----------------------------------------
172.25.12.6
Console> (enable)
```

Listing 5-6 has an additional configuration statement, set ntp broadcastdelay, that adjusts the broadcast delay for the server from the default value of 3,000 microseconds to the value specified with the command (5,000 in Listing 5-6).

Basic Juniper Router NTP Configuration

At its core, the JUNOS software—the OS for Juniper Networks routers—is based on Unix. Since by now you are already somewhat familiar with the Unix NTP configuration statements as well as with some of their counterparts on Cisco routers, the basic Juniper configuration might appear like a rerun. But that's the nature of NTP! It's pervasive, and it's based on the same standards with varying levels of implementation and cosmetic differences in syntax. Listing 5-8 shows basic Juniper virtual router NTP configuration. JUNOS supports the concepts of a virtual router (VR) and virtual routing and forwarding (VRF) instances that exist in the context of a VR. The idea behind a VRF is to have multiple routers within a single physical chassis, which is made even easier through the use of subinterfaces.

Listing 5-8. *Basic Juniper NTP Configuration*

```
host3(config)#virtual-router Apress
host3:Apress(config)#ntp server enable
host3:Apress(config)#ntp server 192.168.6.8
host3:Apress(config)#ntp enable
```

The preceding basic configuration allows the virtual router Apress to act as a server to other clients while it is also a client of an NTP server with an IP address of 192.168.6.8. JUNOS supports broadcast clients, authentication, and access control with respect to NTP.

NTP Security Features

NTP security features include access control and authentication. Both features are inherent to NTP, with access control being typically further augmented by the capabilities of the operating system of an NTP device. NTPv3 supports cryptographic authentication using secret keys (private cryptography), with NTPv4 and SNTP further extending the crypto authentication support via the Autokey protocol while maintaining backward compatibility with NTPv3. The following are examples of NTP security configurations on several categories of devices from different vendors.

CHAPTER 5 ■ NTP DESIGN, CONFIGURATION, AND TROUBLESHOOTING   **117**

NTP Security in Unix/Linux Environments

The restrict command, along with a series of optional parameters, is used to maintain NTP access control in the Unix/Linux environments. The exact syntax of the command is as follows:

```
Restrict IP_address [mask IP_address_mask | default] [param1 param2 param3 …]
```

See the preceding "Typical Unix/Linux Client Configuration" section for an explanation of some of the commonly used parameters that are available with the restrict command. When the IP_address parameter is used without specifying the mask, the mask defaults to 255.255.255.255 (FF.FF.FF.FF in hex or a /32 using the "slash" designation and in this case indicating that all of the bits in the mask are set).

The NTP daemon executes a "logical AND" operation on the incoming source address and the mask, as well as on the IP_address value and the mask, and then compares the two results. If the results are equal, then a match is found. However, just because a match is found does not mean that the restrictions imposed by the parameter list for that particular restrict command entry are going to apply to the incoming packet. Multiple matches are possible for an incoming source address. In the event that multiple matches are found, the parameters associated with the most specific match will apply.

> **Note** The xntpd/ntpd daemon maintains a restriction list that's sorted by the IP address/mask combination, which means that the least specific combination such as 0.0.0.0/0.0.0.0 would be at the top of the list. The daemon searches the list for matches from top to bottom. The last match that's found defines the restrictions that are associated with the parameter values. The last match represents the most specific match or a match on the largest number of bits in the mask.

Consider Listing 5-9, which accentuates the high level of access control granularity that's possible through the use of the restrict command.

Listing 5-9. *Illustration of Access Control Granularity Through the Use of the* restrict *Command*

```
Restrict default nomodify noquery noserve
Restrict 192.168.0.0 mask 255.255.0.0 nomodify noquery
Restrict 192.168.3.0 mask 255.255.255.0 nomodify
Restrict 192.168.3.1
```

For an NTP client that's configured as illustrated in Listing 5-9, an incoming packet with the source address of 192.168.3.1 is going to experience four matches. The first match results from the default policy that matches all incoming NTP-related packets and imposes the most restrictive access policy on them (nomodify, noquery, noserve). The second match that results from the 192.168.0.0 and 255.255.0.0 combination is less restrictive than the default, but it is not the most specific match for this packet. It is only 16 bits long.

The third match is even less restrictive than the second, but it is still not the most specific match for this packet, as it is only 24 bits long. The last match has no restrictions associated with it (the restrict command without any parameters), and because the match is on the full 32 bits of the incoming address, it is the match that the NTP daemon will use to determine what restrictions will apply to this particular packet. In the preceding example, there will be none, since the restrict command that's used only with an IP address and no other parameters imposes no restrictions on the incoming packets that match the source address.

Note Note the high level of granularity in access control that's possible with the use of the restrict command.

NTP authentication in Unix/Linux environments can be configured from the command line, or the xntpd/ntpd daemon can be started with the -k switch to read the contents of the ntp.keys file. The NTP authentication procedure requires a combination of a key and a key identifier. Additionally, the key identifiers must be flagged as trusted in order for them to be usable in time synchronization exchanges. The structure of the ntp.keys file as shown in Listing 5-10 consists of multiple lines that include three fields on each line: key identifier or key number, key type, and actual key.

The key number or identifier is a positive integer in the range from 1 to 2 * 32 – 1. Each entry in the ntp.key file must have a unique key number that's associated with the actual secret key.

When NTP version 3 was originally specified in 1992, it supported the Data Encryption Standard (DES) for the purpose of cryptographic authentication among clients, servers, and peers. DES has since been replaced by the Message Digest 5 (MD5) algorithm. While it's still possible to find NTP implementations that support both DES and MD5 algorithms, support for MD5 has become more common. Consequently, even though the ntp.keys file has a "key type" field to support different key formats (ASCII and hexadecimal, via designations of S, N, and A) and through the "key type" field also to identify the authentication algorithm that would be used, expect most ntp.keys files to have the "key type" field of M for MD5 and the actual key specified in ASCII format, as shown in Listing 5-10.

Listing 5-10. *Structure of the* ntp.keys *File*

```
10          M          MyfirstK
100         M          MysecK
101         M          My3rdK
1000        M          My4thK
```

The definition of keys in the ntp.keys file does not mean they are going to be used. They have to be configured as trusted for the purposes of time synchronization, and the key identifiers then need to be used with server and peer commands.

NTP Security on Cisco Routers and Switches

The syntax of the NTP configuration on Cisco routers and switches varies somewhat from that of the Unix/Linux environments. The principles of the configuration, however, are similar. In place of the restrict command, Cisco allows for the definition of access control lists (ACLs) that can be applied to specific interfaces to control NTP-related traffic. Both standard and extended IP access lists can be used for that purpose depending on the level of access control granularity that is required. Standard IP access lists allow for filtering on the source addresses, while the extended IP access lists filter on source and destination addresses as well as protocols and ports. ACLs can be applied to interfaces for incoming and outgoing traffic.

ACLs are applied to interfaces via the ip access-group command, or they are applied in the global configuration mode via the ntp access-group command to affect the type of associations that are formed between the devices. Listing 5-11 illustrates several commands that are typically used to configure NTP access control on Cisco routers and switches.

Listing 5-11. *NTP Access Control Configuration on a Cisco Router*

```
Router#configure terminal
Enter configuration commands, one per line.  End with CNTL/Z.
Router(config)#interface Serial0
Router(config-if)#ntp disable
Router(config-if)#exit
Router(config)#access-list 199 deny udp any eq 123 any eq 123
Router(config)#access-list 199 permit ip any any
Router(config)#interface Serial1
Router(config-if)#ip access-group 199 in
Router(config-if)#exit
Router(config)#access-list 55 permit host 192.168.1.51
Router(config)#access-list 55 permit host 192.168.10.151
Router(config)#access-list 55 permit host 192.168.100.251

Router(config)#access-list 77 permit 172.16.0.0 0.0.255.255
Router(config)#access-list 77 permit 172.18.1.0 0.255.255.255
Router(config)#access-list 77 permit 192.168.3.0 0.255.255.255
```

```
Router(config)#ntp server 192.168.1.51 version 3
Router(config)#ntp server 192.168.10.151 version 3
Router(config)#ntp server 192.168.100.251 version 3

Router(config)#ntp access-group ?
  Peer              Provide full access
  query-only        Allow only control queries
  serve             Provide server and query access
  serve-only        Provide only server access
Router(config)#

Router(config)#ntp access-group peer 55
Router(config)#ntp access-group serve-only 77
```

Listing 5-11 illustrates the following aspects of NTP access control on a Cisco router:

- Disabling of NTP exchanges over a specified interface via the ntp disable command.

- Screening of the incoming NTP packets via an extended IP access control list, list 199 in the example. List 199 is first defined and then applied to an interface via an ip access-group command. This method relies on the generic capabilities of Cisco's ACLs to deny incoming NTP traffic.

- Using a standard IP ACL to identify NTP servers and then allowing those servers to peer with this host. This is accomplished through the combination of defining a standard IP ACL 55 and then applying the ACL in the ntp access-group command that's used with the peer parameter. Once the access-group command is used with the peer parameter, it means that this router will peer only with those timeservers that are matched by the ACL that's referenced with the command, i.e., 55 in the example. When no ntp access-group command is used, any timeserver can attempt to peer with this router with no restrictions whatsoever. However, whether an active or passive symmetric mode results will depend on whether peer statements are also configured on this router.

- Using a standard ACL to identify networks that can use this router as their server. This is accomplished through the combination of IP ACL 77 and the use of the ntp access-group command with the serve-only parameter. In Listing 5-11, hosts from subnets 172.16.0.0, 172.18.1.0, and 192.168.3.0 will be able to use this router as a timeserver. Whether it's a good idea from a design point of view is not the issue that's being addressed here!

The next configuration example, Listing 5-12, illustrates the process of configuring authentication on Cisco high-end Catalyst switches—models that range from the older 5500 to current mainstream 6500 series units. The configuration is via the switch software as opposed to from the IOS that's also available on the Multilayer Switch Feature Cards (MSFCs) that reside on a switch supervisor engine. The switch software confirms each configuration command.

Listing 5-12. *NTP Client Authentication Configuration on a Cisco Switch*

```
Console> (enable) set ntp key 33 trusted md5 Apress_key
NTP key 33 added
Console> (enable) set ntp server 172.25.12.6 key 33
NTP server 172.25.12.6 with key 33 added.
Console> (enable) set ntp client enable
NTP Client mode enabled
Console> (enable) set ntp authentication enable
NTP authentication feature enabled
Console> (enable) show ntp
Current time: Sat Dec 10 2005, 22:15:25
Timezone: '', offset from UTC is 0 hours
Summertime: '', disabled
Last NTP update: Sat Dec 10 2005, 22:14:53
Broadcast client mode: disabled
Broadcast delay: 3000 microseconds
Client mode: enabled
Authentication: enabled
NTP-Server                                Server Key
----------------------------------------- ---------------
172.16.52.65                                    33
Key Number              Mode     Key String
---------------         ---------  --------------------------------
33                      trusted    Apress_key
Console> (enable)
```

Cisco NTP authentication configuration requires the use of several commands and two key-related parameters. The parameters represent the secret key and the key identifier. RFC 1305 identifies these parameters as the cryptographic key and the key identifier. The NTP authentication procedure requires that the combination of the key and the key identifier match between any NTP devices performing synchronization. The ntp authentication-key command links the secret key and the key identifier. The key identifier is then used as a parameter with the trusted-key and with the server or peer command to allow this host to authenticate its NTP exchanges with its servers or peers. The key identifier must be a

number, while the secret key can be an alphanumeric string. Multiples of the ntp
authentication-key and ntp trusted-key commands are allowed in Cisco configurations
to facilitate redundant authenticated servers and/or peers.

Listing 5-13 demonstrates the configuration of authentication on Cisco routers.
Router1 is a client of Router4. The show ntp associations detail command at the end of
the example illustrates that the synchronization exchanges between Router1 (client) and
Router4 (NTP server that's configured as the local "master") are authenticated.

Listing 5-13. *NTP Authentication Configuration on a Cisco Router*

```
Router1#conf t
Enter configuration commands, one per line.  End with CNTL/Z.
Router1(config)#ntp authentication-key 22 md5 Apress_key
Router1(config)#ntp authenticate
Router1(config)#ntp trusted-key 22
Router1(config)#ntp source serial0
Router1(config)#ntp server 172.16.21.1 key 22
Router1(config)#^Z
Router1#
Router4#conf t
Enter configuration commands, one per line.  End with CNTL/Z.
Router4(config)#ntp authentication-key 22 md5 Apress_key
Router4(config)#ntp authenticate
Router4(config)#ntp trusted-key 22
Router4(config)#^Z

Router1#show ntp associations detail
172.16.21.1 configured, authenticated, our_master, sane, valid, stratum 8
ref ID 127.127.7.1, time C745D7EF.B258F1CC (22:40:47.696 UTC Sat Dec 10 2005)
our mode client, peer mode server, our poll intvl 64, peer poll intvl 64
root delay 0.00 msec, root disp 0.03, reach 377, sync dist 5.661
delay 9.75 msec, offset -2.7284 msec, dispersion 0.76
precision 2**19, version 3
org time C745D815.02640D80 (22:41:25.009 UTC Sat Dec 10 2005)
rcv time C745D815.0456D293 (22:41:25.016 UTC Sat Dec 10 2005)
xmt time C745D815.018EACBC (22:41:25.006 UTC Sat Dec 10 2005)
filtdelay =    9.75    9.75    9.78    9.83   10.16    9.80    9.83    9.77
filtoffset =  -2.73   -2.22   -1.95   -1.37   -1.45   -1.22   -1.42   -2.03
filterror =    0.02    0.99    1.97    2.94    3.92    4.90    5.87    6.85
Router1#
```

Redundant NTP Time Sources

The issue regarding redundant NTP time sources is not so much whether to have them but rather how many of them to have and how to configure redundancy on different types of NTP devices. The concept of redundancy of NTP time sources could be reduced to the following:

- **Redundancy between peers:** This redundancy is at the top of the NTP hierarchy and applies to redundant primary timeservers or to secondary timeservers peering with one another after deriving their time from multiple public servers. Figures 5-5 and 5-6 illustrate this redundancy.

- **Redundancy configuration on clients**: This redundancy applies along the leaves of the NTP hierarchy and is viewed from each client's perspective.

The decision regarding how many redundant time sources to deploy and/or configure will be driven by the factors used to determine the type of time sources in use, as choosing the time source(s) is the first and most critical step in the NTP design process. No absolute formulas exist regarding the number of redundant time sources. But there are some basic, commonsense rules of thumb that stem from the principles of network design.

If you decide it's worth it to have a dedicated private timeserver, chances are that you place sufficient importance on the issues of time accuracy, time source availability, and security that you should probably consider having at least two of them for redundancy. In installations where there are redundant data centers to facilitate business continuity in the event of major infrastructure failures, consider having NTP redundancy at both centers. With two data centers and two timeservers at each center, the four timeservers could be configured for full-mesh peering (each timeserver would act as a peer to the other three), resulting in each timeserver having three redundant time sources. If you wanted to take this process a step further, then each of the timeservers could also be configured with a backup public stratum 1 timeserver, as well as be equipped and configured with an optional internal oscillator to be used in the event of failure of the primary reference time distribution link, i.e., loss of radio or GPS signals. Figure 5-5 illustrates the concept of redundancy among primary timeservers.

For deployments relying on public timeservers, the issue of redundancy is coupled with guarding against the falsetickers. While the redundancy purely from the perspective of the availability of the primary time sources, i.e., the public servers, could well be accommodated with the configuration on the secondary servers of only two or three of the public servers, guarding against falsetickers is best addressed by having somewhere between four and seven public timeservers configured on the secondary (on your LAN) servers. Thus, a redundant NTP deployment that uses Internet public timeservers would have two or three clients (from the perspective of the public servers) that peer with one another (they are the time source to the rest of the clients on the LAN) and are configured

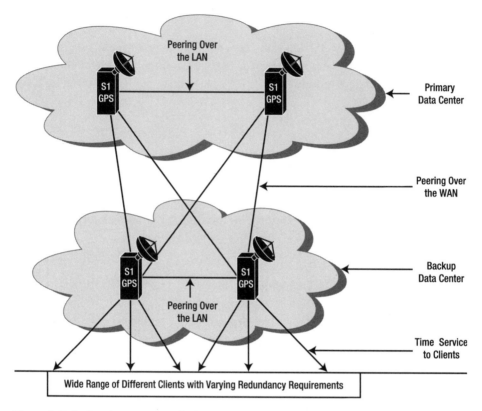

Figure 5-5. *Redundant private dedicated timeservers*

with four timeservers from the Internet. Figure 5-6 illustrates the concept of redundancy among peers (secondary servers) that are using Internet timeservers as their primary time source.

Deployments that rely exclusively on local "masters" could adopt the redundancy concept similar to that used with the primary dedicated timeservers illustrated in Figure 5-5. The big difference would be the issue of time accuracy, as the local "masters" would effectively impersonate the primary time sources.

NTP Operational Modes

The NTP operational modes result from the choices made regarding NTP topology and the subsequent configuration. From the network administration ("net admin") perspective, the specific NTP operational modes fall into the "net admin" mode categories in Table 5-2, which also relates the modes to various configuration commands. The configuration commands listed in Table 5-2 are derived from different operating systems. The

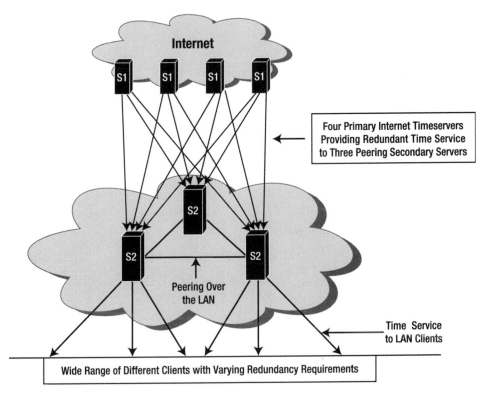

Figure 5-6. *Redundant secondary timeservers*

do not include parameters and are intended only as representative commands to link the "net admin" mode categories and the actual operational NTP modes as defined in RFCs 1305 and 2030.

Table 5-2. *NTP Operational Modes from the "Net Admin" Perspective*

"Net Admin" Mode Category	NTP Operational Modes	Configuration Commands
Peering (think: timeserver redundancy from the topology perspective!)	Symmetric active, symmetric passive	Peer
Client/server point-to-point (think: configuring specific IP address of servers on the clients!)	Client, server	Server
Client/server point-to-multipoint and/or multipoint-to-point (think: enabling broadcasting or multicasting on servers and clients!)	Broadcast, multicast, manycast/anycast	Broadcastclient enable, broadcast client, NTP multicast (on servers), multicast client (on clients)

Additional NTP Configuration Options

Additional NTP configuration options exist above and beyond configuring the basic NTP operations and security. These options include limiting the number of associations for peers, flagging one of the servers or peers as being preferred, adjusting minimum and maximum polling rates, and adjusting the broadcast delay on clients receiving synchronization from a server that's configured to operate in a broadcast mode. Time to Live (TTL) is also adjustable for multicast operations, which effectively allows an administrator to define the diameter of NTP on the network, or how far the multicast NTP packets are going to travel as the TTL counter is decreased each time a packet goes through a router. Not all of the options are going to be available in all of the NTP implementations, given how pervasive the need is for timekeeping and how wide is the range of devices and operating systems that may need time synchronization. In the context of the overall approach to configuration, the optional features come last, as outlined in the following configuration "approach" list:

1. **Basic configuration**: This allows you to ensure that NTP is operational. When configuring any networking protocol in general, ensure that it is operational at the most basic level before proceeding with the configuration of security and optional features.

2. **Security configuration**: Configuring access control and authentication is prone to errors. Incorrect use of masks or parameters in access control configuration can prevent NTP packets from reaching their intended targets despite your good intentions. When it comes to authentication, secret keys and key identifiers must match between communicating devices. If the basic NTP operation already works and adding security features stops it from working, you know where the problem lies.

3. **Optional features**: After basic NTP operations and security have been configured, it's time to tweak the configuration with any optional features.

Step 4: Monitoring and Managing NTP Operations

The approach taken to monitor and manage NTP operations is bound to be directly proportional to the level of importance that is ascribed to NTP functions (accurate and synchronized timekeeping!) by a network administrator and his or her management. Consider that however absolutely critical NTP might be in some networking environments, there are networks out there where NTP is not even configured. The issue of NTP management becomes nonexistent in those scenarios.

Assuming that NTP is configured and operational, consider the decisions you've made regarding the NTP time source, deployment topology, and configuration, i.e., the preceding three steps in the approach to NTP design and configuration. Consider next that the NTP management tools are inextricably coupled with the computing platforms on which the service runs, the level of the overall network management that's already in place, and the optional features you've configured.

With a single dedicated timeserver, you will rely on the device management software that's supplied by the vendor with that timeserver. Additionally, the timeserver could be integrated via SNMP into an overall network management scheme that you may already have in place. With a Unix stratum 2 server serving time to your network clients and itself relying on public stratum 1 servers, you will first and foremost want to ensure that the public servers continue to be available. A periodic automated ping (not every ten seconds but maybe once or twice a day), with an alert e-mail if the ping fails, might be in order. Second, you will want to configure your Unix server to possibly collect NTP-related statistics for troubleshooting any specific NTP problems. With a router acting as a local "master," use the available router and/or network management software to ensure that the router remains up and if it fails that its time does not default to a weird value of decades in the past. If router logs reflect any configuration changes, verify that NTP configuration has not been altered by mistake.

While the preceding sections of this chapter have defined a three-step approach to NTP design and configuration, most of the remainder of this chapter deals with the application of that approach to different size networks. Additionally, the sections consider issues related to networks with or without Internet access, different desktop platforms, and NTP troubleshooting. When you combine the decisions made during the design and configuration steps with the specificity of the available tools on the platforms and in scenarios to which the design/configuration approach has been applied, the result is a unique approach to NTP management that stems directly from this process.

NTP Deployment on Networks with and without Internet Access

The choices regarding NTP deployment on networks with or without Internet access are very clear when you begin with step 1 in the approach to NTP design and configuration process, which is choosing your time source(s). Networks with Internet access have the option of using public servers, while networks without Internet access do not. Given the pervasive reach and the availability of Internet service, it might seem silly for any network not to have Internet access. However, security consideration for some networks may be so stringent that any kind of physical connectivity to the Internet is simply not an option, despite the Internet service availability. And even if there is physical connectivity to the Internet via a firewall, NTP packets might have to be blocked from passing onto the internal network as part of an internal security policy. NTP time source choices for networks without Internet access thus include

Stratum 1 primary timeservers: These could be dedicated timeservers such as Symmetricom's NTS-200 unit shown in Figure 5-1 or multipurpose Unix servers that integrate a primary reference clock.

Stratum 2 or higher devices: These are the local "masters" or impersonators. Routers, switches, and various operating system servers that do not support primary reference clocks, including a Windows 2003 server without any third-party software to turn it into a primary timeserver, could be used in that capacity. That's provided they have the option of being configured as "master" devices. The net effect of utilizing this option without the presence of dedicated timeservers is that time synchronization throughout the network is possible but without accurate reference to UTC.

NTP time sources for networks with Internet access include the preceding choices with the additional option of using public servers (stratum 1, stratum 2, or NTP pool servers).

NTP Deployment Guidelines for Small, Medium, and Large Networks

The rule-of-thumb formula for ascribing a size to a business is based on the number of employees. Small businesses are generally considered to have fewer than 100 employees, medium-size businesses between 100 and 500, and large businesses more than 500. For the purpose of presenting guidelines for NTP deployment, similar criteria are adopted but with respect to devices participating in NTP synchronization rather than employees. The implication is clear. The business size is not even a critical factor as far as NTP deployment guidelines. A large business with more than 500 employees could have a dozen or fewer devices participating in NTP. Similarly, a small business that's leveraging technology rather than people could have 500+ NTP devices. What ultimately matters is the need for accurate and synchronized timekeeping within the business operation.

Note The issue of business size when translated into the number of NTP devices relates to step 2, deciding upon NTP topology at the deployment site; see the section "The Number of NTP Clients" in the four steps to the approach of NTP design and configuration outlined earlier in this chapter.

From the perspective of network management (for any size network!), the natural recommendation regarding NTP is that all computing devices on the network remain synchronized in time for the reasons discussed earlier in this chapter. However, identifying what devices will participate in NTP is ultimately a network design decision driven by business requirements. The NTP deployment guidelines are developed using the four steps identified in the section "Approach to NTP Design and Configuration."

Small NTP Networks

Assume a network with 80 devices in need of time service. The ratio of internal servers to end-user devices is approximately 1:20.

1. **Time source**: Multiple (four to seven) public servers. This decision addresses the issue of redundancy and guarding against falsetickers within the established guidelines for the use of public timeservers. Naturally, the potential for inaccuracy, loss of availability, and security breaches resulting from the use of public timeservers is insufficient to sway the decision in the direction of the use of a dedicated timeserver.

2. **Topology**: Out of the 80 client devices, 4 (internal servers: Unix, Windows, Novell) can act as the stratum 2 servers receiving synchronization from the public servers. The physical topology is LAN only without any WAN links. Having four stratum 2 servers on the LAN is deemed sufficiently redundant for the remaining clients.

3. **Configuration**: Consider access control on the stratum 2 servers with respect to actions from the public servers. Additionally, peering could be established among the stratum 2 servers. The remaining clients could synchronize with one or more of the stratum 2 servers, or they could be configured to receive broadcast/multicast updates from the servers. There does not seem to be much need here for authentication configuration given a single LAN and no WAN links.

4. **Management**: Ensure that public servers remain available. A utility that executes a periodic ping (once or twice a day, not every ten seconds!) to a public server to make sure the server is still around could save headaches resulting from public servers becoming unavailable over a period of time. Perform an occasional "sanity check" of time on the four stratum 2 servers.

Medium-Size NTP Networks

Assume a network with 400 devices in need of time service. A similar ratio of internal servers of 1:20 to end-user devices applies. Additionally, there are multiple WAN links, which implies the use of routers. The interconnected LANs rely on switches capable of acting as NTP stratum 2 servers or higher.

1. **Time source(s)**: Two dedicated timeservers with several public servers acting as backups. The requirements for accuracy and time service availability led to the decision to deploy dedicated timeservers.

2. **Topology**: Take advantage of the reliability and throughput of the dedicated time-servers, and consider a completely flat topology with all of the clients receiving their time directly from the two dedicated timeservers. That will also simplify step 3, which relates to configuration. It is not be advisable to have 400 clients from a single business getting their time directly from the public servers. However, dedicated timeservers are capable of supporting thousands of clients (assuming a certain distribution of the service over time), so having 400 clients is within the usage guidelines.

3. **Configuration**: Configure the dedicated timeservers to peer, and consider operating them either in broadcast mode or in multicast mode. Enable either broadcast or multicast operation on the clients. Configure those clients that are not capable of receiving either broadcast or multicast NTP messages with the addresses of the timeservers. Configure peers to authenticate with one another.

4. **Management**: Use the management software that comes with the timeservers.

Large NTP Networks

When it comes to large networks, the principle of modularity could be applied to consider them as consisting of a number of smaller (small and medium-size) segments. The same approach that applies to NTP deployments on either a small network or a medium-size network could then be applied to the different segments of a large one. If, however, a large network is viewed in a monolithic fashion as a single entity rather than a collection of smaller segments, consider the following approach as it is applied to an enterprise with about 6,000+ devices in need of NTP service:

1. **Time source(s)**: A dozen of dedicated timeservers distributed throughout the enterprise in three clusters of four, each cluster serving about 2,000 other clients.

2. **Topology**: All timeservers within each cluster peer with one another in a full-mesh logical topology. One out of the four timeservers in each cluster has been designated to represent that cluster for the purpose of peering with the other two clusters. Figure 5-7 shows the logical topology for all of the timeservers. The lines between any two timeservers represent a peering relationship. Synchronization service to clients is not shown graphically, but imagine hundreds of lines extending from each S1 timeserver to represent the synchronization exchanges. The clusters of timeservers are physically distributed throughout the enterprise to minimize latency between them and their clients.

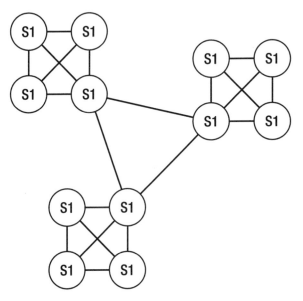

Figure 5-7. *Sample logical topology of dedicated stratum 1 timeservers for a large NTP deployment*

3. **Configuration**: Configure peering and authentication between the timeservers in each cluster and those representing the clusters. In the context of this deployment, peering implies a symmetric active mode of operation, and as a general rule symmetric mode operations should always be authenticated. Install client software that comes with dedicated timeservers on all of the clients that are to synchronize with them. Configure the clients to synchronize with one or more timeservers in two out of the three different clusters.

4. **Management**: Use management software that typically comes with dedicated timeservers. Configure SNMP that can produce e-mail alarms for errors and alerts.

Use of NTP Within the Network Infrastructure

The main function of the network infrastructure devices (routers and switches) is to support fast traffic flow between the network servers and their users. While almost without exception routers and switches from different vendors will support some implementation of NTP (SNTP for the access-level or lower-end devices), the NTP functionality has been built into those devices primarily with the idea of having them act as NTP clients. Try looking for a router or a switch that supports a radio or an atomic clock! Good luck! That trend may be coming, but it's not here yet!

Since routers and switches are not configurable as true stratum 1 servers (with the exception of one acting as the local "master" if the OS supports that function), either those devices act as clients at the very bottom of the NTP hierarchy or they act as secondary servers. In their capacity as secondary servers, they typically receive time synchronization from a primary timeserver or from one of their own colleagues that's configured with a lower stratum number.

However, the fact that routers and switches do not make the best and most reliable timeservers does not diminish that they need to be synchronized in time if the logging activity on the network is going to have any integrity whatsoever. And network administrators are very conscious of how critical accurate logs are when there is a failure, security breach, or intermittent connectivity problem that needs to be resolved. From the network administration perspective, it is thus critical that routers and switches be configured as NTP clients, regardless of whether they additionally act as secondary servers to other clients.

Use of NTP in the Desktop Environment

It seems natural that the desktop computing environment is on the receiving end of the NTP synchronization services, or basically represents the NTP clients. After all, the desktop environment is a lot less stable than the network infrastructure (routers and switches) or server environments that tend to be isolated and protected from accidental shutdowns and user intrusion. And NTP server availability is a serious consideration in the process of choosing your NTP time source. Having said that, consider that with the addition of third-party software and GPS clocks, even common desktop operating systems such as Windows NT, 2000, or XP could turn into primary timeservers.

■Tip For more information about desktop timeservers, visit Galleon Systems' website at http://www.ntp-time-server.com.

While a workstation may not be optimal as a time source for other devices, if a workstation's operational requirements are such that it cannot rely on securing accurate time over the network, then consider equipping such a workstation with its own reference clock and appropriate software to integrate the clock into the workstation's operating system.

Microsoft Windows Workstations and Servers

Microsoft workstation and server software operating systems do not by default support primary reference clocks. However, in a similar manner to routers and switches, Microsoft servers are capable of operating at stratum level 2 or higher and offering time service to other devices throughout the network. It's not unusual to configure the primary domain controller to obtain its time from a primary timeserver and then distribute it to clients throughout the domain. Time synchronization on Microsoft servers (Windows 2003, for example) is implemented via the Windows Time service (W32Time). Be mindful, though, that the Windows Time service does not support synchronization from broadcast or multicast peers. Client devices with a more critical need for accurate time should be pointing to a local timeserver, even if it is a stratum 2 server. Other client devices with access to the Internet could point to `http://time.windows.com` for its time, which is the default configuration for workstations not configured to join a domain.

Unix/Linux Workstations and Servers

The various Unix/Linux OSs are probably the most flexible in terms of NTP support. They facilitate the configuration of primary timeservers, higher-stratum servers, and end-user clients. The primary NTP program remains the `xntpd/ntpd` daemon. The other commonly used programs in these environments are listed in Table 5-3 in the subsequent "NTP-Related Programs and Utilities" section.

The `xntpd/ntpd` daemons support peering, client/server point-to-point (symmetric active mode), and client/server point-to-multipoint (broadcasting and multicasting) NTP operations. While the NTP configuration process and integration of reference clock drivers into the daemons might be more of a challenge in the Unix/Linux environments as compared to that of dedicated timeservers or third-party add-ons to Novell or Windows 2003 servers, the flexibility of configuration and opportunity for fine-tuning remain strong points in these environments. That's provided you are able to allocate the necessary time to those tasks!

Troubleshooting NTP Operations

NTP is a TCP/IP application service. If you suspect a problem with NTP, consider that the lower layers on your TCP/IP network must be functional before you can get into troubleshooting an application service. If an NTP client device is experiencing IP connectivity problems, then chances are its time will also begin to drift. A common approach to troubleshooting any network problem is to start at the physical layer and work your way up. But troubleshooting doesn't have a silver-bullet formula. It takes both systems and experience to be successful at it. Your approach to troubleshooting NTP will also vary greatly as a function of network management procedures and the type of network management system (NMS) that's in place on your network. Assuming that the lower layers of the network are functioning well, here are specific tips for dealing with NTP problems:

- **Become familiar with the functions of all the NTP-related programs and utilities**: The names of the NTP-related programs may vary from one vendor to another, but given the pervasiveness of NTP, a pattern emerges with respect to program/utility functionalities.

- **Use NTP configuration options to your advantage**: Optional NTP parameters can be used to minimize NTP problems that might result from an underlying network problem. Additionally, specific NTP problems can be reported either to a central NMS or via e-mail if SNMP has been properly configured.

NTP-Related Programs and Utilities

In the network infrastructure environments (routers and switches), it's the show and debug commands that allow for the monitoring of individual NTP devices following their configuration. The show commands allow for the display of NTP status and associations, while the debug commands allow for identification of potential problems with synchronization, including those related to authentication. The Linux/Unix environments offer a series of programs and utilities, as defined in Table 5-3, that facilitate not only the operations but also the administration and management of NTP servers in those environments.

Table 5-3. *Linux/Unix NTP-Related Programs and Utilities*

Program Name	Program Description
ntpd/xntpd	The NTP daemon. This program relies on the configuration statements within the ntp.conf, ntp.drift, and ntp.keys files to keep the server on which it is installed synchronized and its communications secure with the configured time source(s). The daemon operates on a server that's configured as a primary timeserver with a reference clock, or the daemon operates on an NTP client with the time source being a primary timeserver or even a high-level stratum server.
ntpq	The NTP query program. The use of the restrict command with the noquery flag within the ntp.conf file can prevent the local host from answering queries from another device that identifies the local host as a parameter (IP address or hostname) in this command. However, this utility is useful when it comes to NTP troubleshooting if the target host permits it. When the command is executed with the name of a target host as a parameter, it allows for subsequent execution of subcommands for display of the peers, NTP associations, clock variables to determine what kind of a clock is used by the timeserver, and more.
ntpdc	A query utility on the order of ntpq but one that uses the mode field value of 7 (instead of 6 for ntpq) in the NTP message header.
ntpdate	A utility that allows the setting of date and time via NTP. This utility can be executed prior to starting the NTP daemon to perform a one-time synchronization with a target server, in case the time on the host machine is significantly off. In the event that an administrator determines that running the NTP daemon poses a potential security risk on a client (you don't have much choice on a primary server!), the ntpdate utility can be periodically executed (run as a CRON job) to maintain the client synchronized with a target server. Don't expect a microsecond accuracy of the host clock with UTC, however, if you decide to use ntpdate as your only time synchronization tool, especially if it's run once a week!
ntptrace	A utility that allows for the tracing of the chain of NTP servers up to the primary time source. This is not unlike the Traceroute utility in TCP/IP that allows for the tracing of a full route to a target host.
ntp-keygen	A program for generating public and private keys that can be used with the Autokey protocol.

The Novell NetWare environments offer programs similar to those of Unix but in the form of NetWare Loadable Modules (NLMs). For example, the NTPQ NLM, which corresponds to the ntpq Unix utility, can be executed to operate in an interactive mode (via the -i switch) with the prompts and then written to and the commands read from the standard output and input, respectively. Associations, peers, and numerous variables can be subsequently displayed and monitored. If synchronization is not working at all, it's advisable to execute the xtnpd/ntpd daemon with a –d flag to enable debugging and to redirect the debugging output to syslog or to standard output (STDOUT).

NTP Configuration with Monitoring and Troubleshooting in Mind

In the Unix/Linux environments, the logging of NTP events is configured by specifying the location of the statistic collection directory in the ntp.conf file and by enabling the writing of the statistics records, which relate to the clock driver, peers, and loop filter statistics. Loop filter is part of the time-server model as specified in RFC 1305's "Determining Time and Frequency" section in Appendix F. Listing 5-14 shows a sample section of the ntp.conf file, illustrating the statistics collection configuration.

Listing 5-14. *Statistics Collection Configuration on* ntp.conf

```
#Define the location and enable the NTP statistics collection
statsdir /var/ntp
statistics loopstats peerstats clockstats
filegen Apress_stats_set file Apress_NTP_stats type week
```

The previous configuration identifies the /var/ntp directory for statistics collection related to the loop filter, the peers, and the clock driver. The filegen command further enables the management of the set of stat files, Apress_stats_set, and characterizes the individual files based on weekly collection intervals (use of the week variable with the type keyword). The reader is referred to each vendor's specific documentation on the subject of configuring NTP statistics collection. In the Novell NetWare environments, the function of statistics collection that is comparable to that shown in Listing 5-14 is accomplished via the XNTPD NLM. The XNTPD NLM offers long-term collection capabilities related to the clock driver, peers, and filter loop statistics. Statistics collection is most likely to be implemented on stratum 1 and 2 servers.

As the NTP hierarchy progresses toward higher stratum levels—from the primary timeservers through the networking infrastructure to the desktop environment—the level of monitoring of NTP operations is bound to diminish. It is critical, however, that as part of routine network management you always ensure the primary timeserver's IP connectivity to the rest of the network. Subsequently, each NTP vendor will or should have management utilities that allow for monitoring the NTP health of the primary timeserver to verify that it continues to offer accurate synchronization service.

Generally, the NTP configurations on secondary servers (whether they be routers, switches, or desktop devices with various OSs) tend to be simpler compared to those of the primary ones. The NTP management of those timeservers might thus be reduced to monitoring their operational ("up") status. As a final configuration tip for routers that are acting as NTP servers, always consider the use of the `ntp source` command to define the IP address that will be used for forming NTP associations. Make the address that of a loopback interface if possible, and, if not, then make the address that of the interface that's considered to be most reliable and least likely to go down.

■■■

NTP: A Journey in Time!

Writing about NTP was a journey in time. Literally! It was a journey that scaled diverse computing environments, science, philosophy, history, and literature, all sharing a common thread: time! On the surface, NTP is simple and almost inconspicuous, overshadowed by many giants inside the TCP/IP suite. As the examples in Chapter 5 reflect, basic configurations involve no more than a few statements. But start digging into it! Before you know, it engulfs you, as it deals with that most fundamental and pervasive element of existence: time! And the science behind it is stunning: atomic clocks, GPS satellites, and complex clock selection and encryption algorithms. And this is all to support the accuracy and distribution of this seeming pervasive and most elusive resource: time!

This book could have been larger! It could have cataloged every NTP implementation on every conceivable networking device and operating system since the protocol's inception. But ironically, in that case the effort would have suffered the ravages of time and never reached the printed page. Thus, what's behind you represents a compromise that time forces all writers to make.

NTP's importance is growing just as the NTP resources available on the Internet are increasing. Yet, it takes time to sift through all those resources and make sense of them all. Thus, the author's hope is that the concentrated journey through NTP's history, architecture, design, and configuration that this publication represents—with pointers to areas that could take up the rest of your life if pursued to the nth degree—has been worth your time. That's especially true if you are one of those network administrators—forward looking in time—who is recognizing the growing importance of maintaining accurate and synchronized time on your networks.

APPENDIX

■ ■ ■

Additional NTP Resources

This appendix consists of references to websites and publications that offer additional resources for further studies on the subject of NTP. Some of these references are mentioned in the main text, while others are not. The websites are categorized by topics related to

- Public NTP servers and pools

- Interplanetary Internet

- NTP version 4 downloads

- Select NTP vendors

- Ongoing NTP research

- Other sites of potential interest

Dedicated publications on the subject of NTP are far and few between. In various networking books, the subject of NTP usually occupies anywhere from a few to a dozen pages. Network operating systems vendors usually have sections on NTP in their product manuals. Some vendors have published white papers on the subject of NTP. Thus, while the volume of publications that reference NTP at some level may be significant, the two key publications that warrant the greatest attention from NTP designers are the latest specifications for NTP version 3 and SNTP. They are listed at the end of the appendix.

Websites

The following are sites dedicated to public servers and pools:

- http://www.eecis.udel.edu/~mills/ntp/clock1b.html

- http://ntp.isc.org/bin/view/Servers/WebHome

- http://www.pool.ntp.org

The following are sites dedicated to the Interplanetary Internet:

- http://computer.howstuffworks.com/interplanetary-internet.htm

- http://www.ipnsig.org/aboutstudy.htm

The following are sites dedicated to NTP version 4 source code and cryptographic libraries:

- http://www.openssl.org/

- http://ntp.isc.org/bin/view/Main/SoftwareDownloads

The following are sites dedicated to select vendors:

- http://www.ntp-systems.com

- http://www.ntp-time-server.com

The following are sites dedicated to ongoing research:

- http://www.ietf.org/html.charters/ntp-charter.html

- https://ntp.isc.org/bin/view/IETF/WebHome

The following are sites dedicated to other miscellaneous NTP-related information:

- http://www.eecis.udel.edu/~mills/ntp/

- http://tycho.usno.navy.mil/leapsec.html

Publications

The following are the two key publications of interest:

- Mills, David L. *RFC 1305, Network Time Protocol (Version 3) Specification, Implementation and Analysis.* Newark: University of Delaware, 1992.

- Mills, David L. *RFC 2030, Simple Network Time Protocol (SNTP) Version 4 for IPv4, IPv6 and OSI.* Newark: University of Delaware, 1996.

Bibliography

Audi, Robert, general editor. *The Cambridge Dictionary of Philosophy*, pbk ed. Cambridge: Cambridge University Press, 1995.

Barnes-Svarney, Patricia, editorial director. *The New York Public Library Science Desk Reference*. New York: Stonesong Press, 1995.

Barnett, Mary. *Gods and Myths of the Romans*. New York: Smithmark Publishers, 1996.

Bergmann, Peter Gabriel. *Introduction to the Theory of Relativity*. With a foreword by Albert Einstein. New York: Dover Publications, 1942.

Cantor, Norman F. *Medieval History: The Life and Death of a Civilization*. New York: Macmillan, 1963.

Corrick, James A. *The Industrial Revolution*. San Diego: Lucent Books, 1998.

Couch, Malcolm. *Greek and Roman Mythology*. New York: Todtri Productions, 1997.

Craig, Edward, editor. *Concise Routledge Encyclopedia of Philosophy*. London: Routledge, 2000.

Durant, Will. *The Life of Greece*. The Story of Civilization: 2. New York: Simon and Schuster, 1939.

Durant, Will. *Caesar and Christ*. The Story of Civilization: 3. New York: Simon and Schuster, 1944.

Durant, Will. *The Age of Faith*. The Story of Civilization: 4. New York: MJF Books, 1950.

Ford, Kenneth William. *The Quantum World, Quantum Physics for Everyone*. Cambridge, MA: Harvard University Press, 2004.

Greene, Brian. *The Elegant Universe: Superstrings, Hidden Dimensions, and the Quest for the Ultimate Theory*, pbk ed. London: Vintage, 1999.

Halliday, David, and Robert Resnick. *Physics Parts I and II*. New York: John Wiley & Sons, 1960.

Harmon, William, editor. *The Top 500 Poems*. New York: Columbia University Press, 1992.

Homer. *The Illiad,* trans. Alston Hurd Chase and William G. Perry Jr. Boston: Little, Brown and Company, 1950.

Past Worlds: Atlas of Archeology. New York: Borders Press, 2003.

Roberts, Timothy R. *Ancient Rome: Chronicles of the Roman World.* n.p.: MetroBooks, 2000.

Ross, Stewart. *The Industrial Revolution.* London: Evans Brothers Limited, 2000.

Sale, Kirpatrick. *Rebels Against the Future: The Luddites and Their War on the Industrial Revolution, Lessons for the Computer Age.* Reading, MA: Addison-Wesley, 1995.

Shakespeare, William. *William Shakespeare: Complete Poems.* New York: Gramercy Books, 1993.

Whittier, John Greenleaf. *Poems of Whittier.* New York: Books, Inc., n.d.

Index

time-dependent operational activities, importance of time synchronization for, 46

timestamps, values of in data messages, 54

Token Ring LAN access method, Sparta vs. Athens as precursor of, 31–32

Token Ring LAN controllers, initial shipment of by IBM, 31

transactional integrity, need for as motivation for NTP deployment on a network, 93

transmit timestamp (64-bit unsigned fixed-point integer) field, in NTP version 3 data messages, 53

Trojan War, networking aspects of, 29–31

Troubleshooting, NTP operations, 133

Truechimer, defined, 91

■U

undisciplined local clock, 109

Universal Solvent (US), application of to the "past" energy states, 35

Unix/Linux clients, basic NTP configuration of, 108–110

Unix/Linux environments
 NTP authentication in, 118
 NTP security in, 117–119

Unix/Linux primary timeserver, basic NTP configuration of, 110–111

Unix/Linux workstations and servers, NTP programs for these environments, 133

U.S. National Institute of Standards and Technology
 call letters for radio stations operated by, 43
 GPS satellite radio station operated by, 43

UTC. *See* Coordinated Universal Time (UTC)

utilities
 ntpdc utility, 51
 ntp-genkeys utility, 85
 ntpq utility, 51

■V

version number (3-bit integer) field, in NTP version 3 data messages, 50–51

Virgil (Roman poet), epic poem *Aeneid* by, 32

■W

W32Time. *See* Windows Time service (W32Time)

Watson, Thomas, Sr., one-time chairman of IBM, 36

website address
 for current release of NTP version 4 source files, 85
 dedicated to ongoing research for NTP, 140
 dedicated to select vendors for NTP, 140
 for information about IPN, 61
 for information about NTP pool servers, 101
 for information about Symmetricom's timeservers, 107
 for OpenSSL library, 85
 for public NTP stratum 1 server information, 48
 for sites dedicated to Interplanetary Internet, 140
 for sites dedicated to NTP version 4 source code and cryptographic libraries, 140
 for sites dedicated to public servers and pools, 139

Western Empire, fall of, 33

Whittier, John Greenleaf, "The New Year" by, 24–25

Windows Time service (W32Time), time synchronization on Microsoft servers with, 132–133

written history period
 vs. Internet-era period, 28
 vs. prehistoric times, 28

■X

Xerox Networking Service (XNS) protocol suite, 32

xntpd/ntpd daemon, drift file maintained by, 110

■Z

Zeus, interest in Thetis daughter of Nereus, 29–30